Musica Asiatica

I

Musica Asiatica
I

Edited by Laurence Picken

Oxford University Press
Music Department, 44 Conduit Street, London W1R 0DE

ISBN 0 19 323234 0

Printed and bound in Great Britain by
The Scolar Press Ltd., Ilkley, Yorkshire

Foreword

Musica Asiatica, conceived as an occasional, periodical publication, is intended (in first place) to make possible publication of extended studies of musical documents from the fields of Asian music, both in transcription and, where appropriate, in original. At the present time, limitations of space would have precluded publication of a majority of the short monographs in this first volume in those few international journals devoted to musicological — and more particularly to ethnomusicological — studies. The occasional placing of such a study in a journal otherwise devoted to oriental (and primarily linguistic, historical, or literary) studies in general, serves only to add to the dispersal of a musicological literature already sufficiently dispersed, thus increasing difficulties of access and study.

A major aim will be to present studies on Asian music so that their results are readily accessible to all scholars in the field of music, no matter whether their interests are majority, 'musicological' interests or those of the kind somewhat artificially distinguished as 'ethnomusicological'. In order to facilitate access, the use of Asian languages and scripts in the body of the text will be reduced to a minimum. The Western reader is *not* expected to acquire an exotic vocabulary before being permitted to catch a glimpse of music; indeed, it is hoped that he will find nothing 'foreign', nothing 'alienating', about the presentation; it is hoped rather that he may be able to look at early 'medieval' musics of East Asia (for example) with no greater sense of cultural shock or even of exclusion than would be experienced, let us say, if the secular repertory of the Court of Charlemagne were suddenly restored to us.

It is our view: that the musics of Asia and Europe constitute a single, historical continuum; that processes of development and evolution observable in one region are relevant elsewhere; that musical evolution in Europe is not to be understood in isolation from that of Asia, any more than evolution in East Asia is to be understood in isolation from processes in Central or Western Asia, in the Ancient Middle East, and more recently in Europe; that throughout Eurasia, the social context of music, indeed, the sociology of music can only be adequately explored on a supranational basis.

It is now plain, and this volume alone would suffice to demonstrate the fact, that the documentation of many aspects of early musical history is substantially fuller, and extends further backwards in time, in Asia than in Europe. This is so for the history of musical forms, of melody types, of secular music in general, as well as for the history of instruments, of instrumental techniques and of instrumental ornamentation. In each of these fields, East Asian documentary sources carry us back to a point in time some five or six centuries earlier than the earliest equivalent European sources. With so great a priority, it would be rash to assert that there can be no possible link between Asian, and especially Central Asian, musics and the music of Europe. We now know, for example, not merely what music was played on East Asian lutes and zithers of the eighth and ninth centuries, but precisely how it was played, with respect both to technique and to ornamentation. We know too what kinds of tunes, and even what tunes, were being played in Kucha, Khotan, Turfan, Qočo, and other oasis-states of Central Asia, in the seventh and eighth centuries. Significantly, perhaps, these tunes are in part strikingly 'western' rather than 'oriental' in character. The potential importance of this fact requires no emphasis.

In this series of volumes, it is planned to include, as they arise, studies of sound-producing devices and of musical instruments, in which all aspects, including physical studies, are combined. The aim here is to encourage increasing awareness of the need to deepen inquiry into the organization and properties of instruments, in the interests of a more ample and more adequate organology. The musical significance of the course of instrumental evolution, and its point-by-point correlation with the evolution of music, are as yet fields of study almost wholly unexplored.

To those who have read thus far, it will come as no surprise that *Musica Asiatica* is conceived as a contribution to the science of Musicology. The hiving-off on grounds of social-scientific emphasis of a field of 'Ethnomusicology' devoted to musics of the *ethne,* may be convenient; but we believe its convenience is temporary only. For the Heartland of Eurasia, there can now be little doubt that the history of music, of musical instruments, and of the relationship of music to culture, is one history. For this one supra-continental landmass, there is one 'musicology', to knowledge of which (it is hoped) *Musica Asiatica* may contribute.

L. E. R. Picken
Jesus College
Cambridge
England

Contents

Acknowledgements

The work of a 'Tang Music Project' sponsored by the American Council of Learned Societies, in which two contributors to this volume participated (R.F.W. and A.J.M.), has in part been financed by a grant from the Andrew Mellon Foundation. Publication has been made possible by a Research Award from The British Academy. We acknowledge with gratitude the help afforded us. We also record gratefully the support given by Prof. Dr. Herbert Franke, University of Münich, Prof. D.C. Twitchett, F.B.A., University of Cambridge, and by the late Prof. Arthur F. Wright, University of Yale. Our appreciative thanks go to Mr. Terence J. Allbright who copied musical examples, to Mr. R.S. Wang who wrote the Chinese and Sino-Japanese texts, and to Mr. M.J. Cartwright, Printing Manager to the University Library, Cambridge, who prepared with such care a volume of some complexity.

Tunes notated in flute-tablature from a Japanese source of the tenth century

A.J. MARETT

(Jesus College, Cambridge)

The flute manuscript *Hakuga fue-fu*[1] (henceforth HFF), completed in 966 by, or under the editorial supervision of, Minamoto no Hiromasa (Hakuga)[2] (919-980), is of the greatest importance for the study of early Sino-Japanese music, since it is one of the oldest surviving[3] collections of tunes from the 'Tang-music' (*Tōgaku*) repertory, that is, the repertory of Chinese court-music of the Tang dynasty (618-905) preserved at the Japanese Court. HFF consisted originally of four scrolls, of which only the fourth now survives; all copies of the manuscript contain the heading, *'Newly Edited Music Scores*: fourth transverse-flute scroll'[4]. All known copies date from the eighteenth century or

1   博雅笛譜 . Alternative titles: *Shinsen gaku-fu* 新撰樂譜 (Newly edited music scores); *Hakuga no sammi no fu* 博雅三位 譜 (Hakuga-of-the-Third Rank's score); *Chōshūkyō no take no fu* 長 秋卿竹譜 (Lord Long-Autumn's bamboo score); *Chōchiku-fu* 長竹 譜 (Long bamboo score); *Hakuga chōchiku-fu* 博雅長竹 譜 (Hakuga's Long bamboo score).

2   源博雅 For further biographical details see Marett, A.J. 'Hakuga's flute score: a tenth-century Japanese source of 'Tang-music' in tablature.' (Doctoral Dissertation, University of Cambridge); E. Harich-Schneider, *A History of Japanese Music* (London, 1973) pp. 191-92.

3   Three 'Tang-music' sources earlier than HFF survive: the *Tempyō biwa-fu* 天平 琵琶譜 of *ca* 750; the *Fushiminomiya bon biwa-fu* 伏見宮本 琵琶譜 of 920/21; the *Gogen-fu* 五絃譜 of 842.

4   新撰樂譜卷第橫笛四

later. For the present study, three late copies have been investigated in microfilm: *Copy A* (microfilm presented to Dr. Picken by Mr. Fukushima Kazuo, Director of the Research Archives for Japanese Music, Ueno Gakuen College): from the 'Rakusaidō Gagaku Manuscripts' (two volumes, catalogue numbers 87, 88) in the Research Archives for Japanese Music, Ueno Gakuen College. This unsigned and undated copy (probably of late Edo date) is a copy of a copy made by Toyohara no Tomoaki[5] in 1731. Mr.Fukushima considers this the best of a number of copies deriving from that of Toyohara no Tomoaki[6]. It is the most accurate of the three copies seen by me. *Copy B* (microfilm obtained with the permission of the Library authorities): an unsigned and undated copy from the Library of the University of the Arts (Geijutsu Daigaku), Tokyo (Catalogue Number 1363.1 16.15.1). *Copy C*: an unsigned and undated copy from the Library of the University of the Arts, Tokyo (Catalogue Number 1183 24/65 16.15.11.1)[7].

In a recently published note on this source, Harich-Schneider[8] comments on the poor condition of a late copy consulted by her. After examination, in the light of the present study, of her transcriptions of three pieces from HFF, it seems, however, that errors in these are the result not so much of flaws in the manuscript as of misinterpretation of the explanation of notational symbols and flute-fingerings that follow the notations in the manuscript, and of imperfect understanding of the distinctive mensural notation employed. A short comment by Garfias seems to suggest that HFF is virtually unintelligible: 'only the taiko stroke of each phrase and the phrase endings are given, and there is no indication of the measures or the beats to the measures'.[9]

In a postface,[10] Hakuga states that his score was compiled from a number of earlier scores, some of which date from the early ninth century. He concludes, 'since then, those who play well have gradually died out. Although they have a reputation of sorts, their skill is inadequate, and all men lament the decline of this way. For this score, however, I have adopted the tablature styles of those times'. Six different tablature-styles have indeed been identified in HFF[11]. It is almost certain that each reflects the style, or more precisely the Notational System, of one or other of Hakuga's sources. Only in one instance, however, has the source of a System been identified. In this present study, two Notational Systems only will be considered; 41 out of a total of 50 pieces in the manuscript

5   豊原 倫秋   1698-1769.

6   This view was expressed in a letter of 6 August, 1975, to Dr. Picken.

7   For further bibliographical details see Marett, op.cit. (see n.2), Chapter I.

8   E. Harich-Schneider, op.cit., pp. 192-213. Transcriptions appear on p. 213.

9   Garfias, R. *'The Tōgaku Style of Japanese Court Music'* (Ann Arbor, 1965) p.267.

10   For an annotated translation see, Marett, op.cit. (see n.2). Chapter II.

11   Marett, op.cit. (see n.2), Chapter II.

are in one or other of these Systems, however. The main difference between the Systems is that System I includes red dots to the left of certain tablature signs, as indicators of overblowing[12], whereas System II does not. (Red dots are transcribed as circles above notes (see p. 27). Certain stylistic differences between pieces in each System, namely, a higher degree of ornamentation and shorter phrase-lengths in pieces in System I than in System II, suggest that pieces in System II are from an earlier source than those in I[13].

TABLATURE SIGNS AND THEIR PITCHES

The notation of pieces in HFF is a tablature. The symbols do not indicate pitches, but finger-positions on a standard transverse flute, with finger-holes I-VII. Towards the end of the manuscript in a section headed 'Notes on the Method of Scoring' all tablature signs are listed, and the least straightforward fingerings are explained. The list of tablature-signs begins:

'Hole [-fingering] names[14]. [II] *kan*[15] 干 ; [III] *go* 五 ; [IV] *jō*[16] 上 ; [V]

shaku[17] 夕 ; [VI] *chū* 中 ; *ge*[18] 丅 ; [VII] *roku* 六 ; [O] *kō*[19] 口 .'

All but two of these tablature-signs (丅 and 口) are the names of

finger-holes. As notational signs they indicate that the hole of the same name, along with all holes distal to the named hole (except in the case of VII), is open.

In the 六 (VII) fingering, all holes distal to the 六 hole are *closed* thus

六 中 夕 上 五 干 之   The meaning of the two signs that are

[12]   Marett, op.cit. (see n.2), Chapter III.

[13]   Marett, op.cit. (see n.2), Chapter III.

[14]   穴 名 : literally 'hole-names', is translated as 'hole [-fingering] names' since two

of the sign listed under this heading do not indicate single, named holes on the flute. Furthermore, the hole-name 之 [I], *not* a tablature-sign in HFF, is not included in the list.

[15]   The correct Chinese form of the lexigraph is 干 .

[16]   Kaichiku-shō 懷 竹 抄 (in Gunsho-ruijū IX) p.89 states, 'the old form of

the lexigraph is 上 '.

[17]   The lexigraph 夕 may be an abbreviation of 名 . The mumei 無 名 finger is

the ring finger. In modern performance practice this finger stops the 夕 [V] hole.

[18]   Kaichiku-shō, p.89 (see n.16) states, 'the old form of the lexigraph is 下 '.

[19]   Also read 'ro'. This reading was given to Dr. Picken by Mr. Ono Setsuryū 小 野

攝 龍 , Director of Music at the Shitennōji, Ōsaka.

3

not hole-names is stated in a passage which follows the list of tablature-signs in

HFF. 丁 is explained as follows: 'Counting from the bottom to the top of the

flute but with the holes 六 [VII] and 夕 [V] open at the same time, on

blowing this yields 丁 [20]' The meaning of this passage becomes clearer in the

light of a diagram in the thirteenth century *Zoku-Kyōkunshō*[21], of which Figure
1 below is a simplified version from which certain details, irrelevant to the
present discussion, have been omitted.

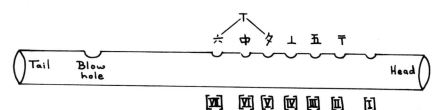

Figure 1: Diagram of transverse flute, modified from original in
Zoku-Kyōkunshō. Finger-holes and tablature-signs. See text, p. 4.

Lines connecting the sign 丁 to the finger-holes VII and V imply that

both holes are open simultaneously while VI remains closed. The 丁 fingering

may be conveniently expressed as (V+VII). The passage describing this fingering
is possibly the earliest textual reference to cross-fingering in any culture.

The final tablature-sign 口 is defined: 'With all stopped, on blowing

[this] is called the [O] kō hole[-fingering].'[22] One finger-hole on the flute

is not used as a tablature-sign (see n. 14), namely I. HFF notes, 'The hole below
II is called the *shi* hole. It is used with II.'[23] The late thirteenth century text,
Kaichiku-shō (henceforth KCS), in the tradition of the flute-master Ōga

20 從 下 方 計 至 上 方 但 六 夕 一 度 開 吹 為 下 穴

21 續 教 訓 鈔   In *Nihon Koten Zenshū* (henceforth NKZ) (Tokyo, 1939)

p.497.

22 皆 塞 抑 吹 名 口 穴

23 于 之 下 穴 名 曰 之 穴 合 用 于 穴

Koresue (1026-1094),[24] explains the function of this hole: 'This is not used separately. It yields the *embai* of II.'[25],[26] Embai, literally, 'salt plums', means 'ornamentation' in a musical context. We may conclude that the most distal finger-hole of the flute was used solely for purposes of ornamentation.

The pitch produced by each of the fingerings is not named in HFF, and for a precise statement of the pitches that correspond to the tablature signs we are dependent on the later KCS: ' 干 [II], 五 [III], 上 [IV], 五 [V], 中 [VI], 丁 [V+VII], 六 [VIII] respectively yield the seven different lengths [= pitch-pipe lengths = absolute pitches]: E (*hyō*), F♯(*shimonu*), G (*sō*,), A (*ōjiki*), B (*banjiki*), C (*kaminu*), and D (*ichi*)'[27] [28] Of the remaining tablature sign, 口 [O], KCS states: 'As to the note of 口 ; its note is the same as that of 六 [VII]' that is, D and: 'the two hole[-fingerings] 口 and 六 are one note in the lower and upper octaves.'[29] [30] That is, *d" and d"'* are produced by different fingerings.[31]

Summarizing the statement in KCS regarding the relationship between tablature signs and pitch:

六	丁	中	夕	上	五	干	口	
D	C♯	B	A	G	F♯	E	D	(lower octave)

The pitches listed in KCS do not include all those required if mode-keys in HFF are to be correctly realised. Pieces are arranged under five headings: 'Pieces

---

[24]   Eckardt, H. *'Das Kokonchomonshū des Tachibana Narisue als Musikgeschichtliche Quelle.* (Wiesbaden, 1956) p.30.

[25]   非 別 當 為 干 塩 梅

[26]   Kaichiku-shō, p. 63.

[27]   干 五 上 夕 中 丁 六 以 如 此 次 為 平 下 双 黄 盤
上 壹 之 七 種 條

[28]   Kaichiku-shō, p. 63.

[29]   口 音 其 音 與 六 同 ; 口 六 二 穴 者 一 音 大 小 合

[30]   Kaichiku-shō, p. 63.

[31]   Harich-Schneider, op.cit., p.211 states, 'it is evident [from the passage in HFF] that the technique of overblowing was well understood'. This is not so: *d'''* is produced, not by overblowing, but by a different fingering.

5

in the Sō[32] mode'; 'Pieces in the Ōjiki[33] mode'; 'Pieces in the Sui[34] mode'; 'Pieces in the Banjiki[35] mode'; 'Pieces in the Kaku[36] mode'. The group headed 'Pieces in the Banjiki mode' contains 20 pieces, the largest number in any group, of which 15 are in Notational Systems I and II. From the twelfth-century lute-manuscript Sango-yōroku[37] (henceforth SGYR) and the zither-manuscript of the same date, Jinchi-yōroku[38] (henceforth JCYR), it is clear that 'Banjiki' refers to a specific mode-key, the Dorian mode on B: B C#D E F#G# A. Studies of Tang modes by both Yang[39] and Picken[40] confirm that this was the character of the equivalent Chinese mode, Banshe[41]. In the notation of pieces in Systems I and II, from the Banjiki modal group, the tablature-sign used for the final (B) is, in all but three instances (see below), 中 . It may be concluded that the fingering indicated by 中 yields the note B, as KCS suggests. The notes implied by all tablature-signs in this mode-key are: 六
D

(VII), 丁 (VII+V), 中 (VI), 夕 (V), 上 (IV), 五 (III), 干 (II). In
    C#   B   A   G#   F#   E
all but one instance, these agree with the pitches listed in KCS; in the Banjiki mode-key, the sign 上 here yields the pitch G#, however, rather than G♮, as suggested in KCS.

In two pieces, 'Sword Vapours', 'The White Pillar', (see pp.51,57) the final is notated by the sign 五 (F#). In these pieces, the mode-key is not Dorian on B, but Aeolian on F# : F# G# A B C# D, that is, although the key (that is, the pitches used) are the same as those of the Banjiki mode-key, the final is different. The mode key of the suite, 'Miss Cao', listed under the heading

32   雙

33   黃鐘

34   水

35   盤涉

36   角

37   三五要錄

38   仁智要錄

39   Yang, Yinliu. *'Zhongguo Yinyue Shigang* 中國音樂史綱 ,
     (Shanghai, 1953) pp.178-86.

40   Picken, L.E.R. 'Tang Music and Musical Instruments' in *T'oung Pao* (1965) pp.92-100.

41   盤涉 (= Banjiki, see n.35).

'Pieces in the Kaku (Aeolian) mode', is also the Aeolian on F♯. In a single suite, 'Liquidamber Incense', the final is notated by the sign 六 (D). The mode-key of this piece is the Lydian on D: D E F♯ G♯ A B C♯. It may be concluded that pieces listed under the heading 'Pieces in the Banjiki mode' include not only the mode-key called Banjiki (Dorian on B), but all modes in the same key as Banjiki — that is, modes using the notes D E F♯ G♯ A B C♯. It is not clear why one piece in this key, namely, 'Miss Cao', appears under a separate heading.

The second largest group of pieces (19, of which 18 are in System I or II) is that under the heading 'Pieces in the Ōjiki mode'. It is clear, both from JCYR and SGYR, that 'Ōjiki' refers specifically to the mode-key Dorian on A: A B C D E F♯ G. Both Yang[42] and Picken[43] confirm this as the character of the equivalent Tang mode-key, Huangzhong[44]. The final (A) of all but one piece in this modal group is notated by the sign 勺. This confirms that, as suggested in KCS (and as was the case for pieces in the Banjiki modal group), the 勺 sign indicates a fingering that yields the note A. The notes implied by all tablature-signs in this mode-key are: 六 (VII), 丅 (VII+V), 中 (VI), 勺
....D............C.............B...........A

(V), ⊥ (IV), 五♯ (III) 干 (II) Except for the pitch implied by the sign
....G..............F♯..........E

丅 , these pitches agree with those given in KCS; 丅 here yields C♮, however, and not the C♯ suggested in KCS. The sign ⊥ , which in the Banjiki modal group yields G♯, here yields G♮.

The final of one piece, 'Pink and White Peach and Plum Blossoms (Broaching)' (see p. 28) is notated not with 勺 (A), but with 干 (E). The mode-key of this piece is Aeolian on E: E F♯ G A B C D, which, according to Picken's reconstruction of the Tang modal system, has the specific name Etsukaku/Yuejiao[45]. 'Pink and White Peach and Plum Blossoms' is included in the Ōjiki modal group because it is in the same key as the Ōjiki mode-key.

The third largest group (four pieces only) is that under the heading, 'Pieces in the Sui mode'. According to SGYR and JCYR, Sui is a Mixolydian mode on A: A B C♯ D E F♯ G. The tablature-sign used in HFF for the final of pieces in this mode-key 勺 (A). No mode-key of this name appears in the source used for Picken's reconstruction of Tang modes, namely, Yuefu zalu[46]. Yang[42] notes

---

[42] Yang, op.cit., p.183.

[43] Picken, op.cit., 1965 p.98.

[44] 黄 鐘 (= Ōjiki, see n.33).

[45] 越 角 The Japanese reading is given first.

[46] 樂 府 雜 錄

that Shui[47] (=Sui) is an alternative name for the Xiezhi[48] mode-key, a Mixolydian mode (as in Japanese practice), but on B — not, as in Japan, on A. As Hayashi[49] points out, it appears that the Sui/Shui mode-key was a tone higher in Chinese practice than in Japanese.

The next group to be considered is that headed 'Pieces in the Sō mode'. This contains four pieces, but only two of these are in System I. From SGYR and JCYR, it is clear that the Sō mode-key, in Japanese usage, is an Ionian mode on G: G A B C D E F♯ . In the Tang system, the Shuang (=Sō) mode-key was Mixolydian, however.[42],[43] Yang shows that Shuang was the Mixolydian mode on G: G A B C D E F♮ . The conversion of F♮ (in Chinese practice), to F♯ (in Japanese practice) probably came about when the mouth-organ (shō[50]) was standardized with a pipe sounding F♯ , but none sounding F♮ . Traynor and Kishibe[51] have suggested that on early Japanese mouth-organs, such as the Kuretake-shō[52], a pipe sounding F (boku[53]) could be substituted when a mode such as the Sō mode was to be played[54]: 'It should be noted that boku would be useful as ei-u [F] of that same mode [i.e., Sō]: its presence would relieve the Shō player of the necessity of substituting henkyu i.e. f♯ for ei-u, i.e. f, a practice which is both inaccurate and unharmonious, and indeed destroys the original mode[55].'

Evidence from the lute-score 'Fushiminomiya-bon biwa-fu[56]' — the surviving copy of which is closer in date (920/21) to HFF (966) than either JCYR or SGYR — suggests that, in Hakuga's time, the correct form of the mode was played, that is with F♮ .[57] This is confirmed by evidence from HFF itself regarding ornamentation in pieces in the Sō mode-key (see p.11). It may be concluded that, in the time of Hakuga, the sign 五 yielded F♮ in the Sō mode-key.

48 歇 指   47 水   (see n.34).

49 Hayashi, K. 'Hakuga fue-fu kō' in *Gagaku* (Tōyō Ongaku Sensho) Tokyo, 1969, p.295.

50 笙

51 Leo Traynor and Shigeo Kishibe, 'The four unknown pipes of the Shō (mouth organ) used in ancient Japanese Court music' in *Tōyō Ongaku Kenkyū IX* (Tokyo, 1951) pp.26-53.

52 呉 竹 笙   : preserved in the Imperial Treasure House (Shōsōin) at Nara.

53 卜

54 Traynor and Kishibe, op.cit., pp.49, 50.

55 Traynor and Kishibe, op.cit., p.35.

56 Wolpert, R.F., 'A ninth-century Sino-Japanese lute tutor' in *Musica Asiatica I* (London, 1977) p. 113).

57 Marett, op.cit., n.2, Chapter III.

Table I: Pitches (Helmholtz pitch-notation) corresponding to tablature-signs in all modal groups in HFF.

Modal groups (keys)	六	丁	中	夕	上	五	丅	口
Banjiki	d‴	c#‴	b″	a″	g#″	f#″	e″	d″
Ōjiki	d‴	c‴	b″	a″	g″	f#″	e″	d″
Sui	d‴	c#‴	b″	a″	g″	f#″	e″	d″
Sō	d‴	c‴	b″	a″	g″	f″	e″	d″
Kaku	d‴	c#‴	b″	a″	g#″	f#″	e″	d″

Table I shows that several tablature-signs imply more than one pitch: 丁 must yield c#‴ in pieces in the Banjiki, Sui and Kaku modal groups, but

c♮‴ in pieces in the Ōjiki and Sō modal groups; 上 must yield g#″ in the

Banjiki and Kaku modal groups, but g♮″ in the Ōjiki, Sui and Sō modal

groups; 五 must yield f#″ in all modal groups except Sō, where it yields

f♮″ . Later textual sources confirm that, in spite of the evidence in KCS, cited above (see p. 4), more than one note may be produced on some finger-holes. In Zoku-kyōkunshō[58], a passage headed, 'The pattern of mouth-organ notes in unison with the five degree-names and the flute hole[-fingerings]' lists the degrees of each mode in three different notations: mouth-organ tablature — an unambiguous pitch notation (since each sign indicates a pipe of fixed pitch), degree-name, and flute-tablature. This shows that the sign 上 implies either

g″ or g#″ , and that the sign 丁 implies either c‴ or c#‴ .

All pieces in HFF were to be played on a single standard flute (and not on a set of flutes in different keys). Hayashi[59] has suggested that when a standard flute was adopted for the performance of Tang-music, so that it became necessary to produce more than one pitch from certain finger-holes, the finger-holes were enlarged to make possible a greater variation in pitch: techniques such as partial covering of finger-holes, or control of wind-pressure, to modify the pitch of a note, are easier to execute on a flute with larger finger-holes. Hayashi's suggestion is supported by the fact that the size of finger-holes on four early flutes (in different keys) preserved in the Shōsōin, is considerably smaller than those on the standard flute now used for 'Tang-music'.

[58] NKZ op.cit., p.360.

[59] Hayashi, op.cit., p.295.

ORNAMENTATION

Among signs listed and defined in the section of HFF headed, 'Notes on the Method of Scoring' (see p.3) are four that appear to be ornaments. They are defined as follows:

(a) ' 由 (yuri): rub the hole with the finger.[60] '

(b) ' 由 リ リ リ : first yuri; afterwards prolong.[61] '

(c) ' リ リ リ 由 : prolong by blowing; afterwards yuri.[62] '

(d) ' 連 (ren): move the finger.[63] '

The sign (c) occurs only in the 'Notes on the Method of Scoring' and not in the body of the manuscript; (d) does not occur in any piece transcribed and will not be discussed here.

The relationship between (a) and (b) and pitch has been studied by Hayashi[64]. From a statistical survey of all pieces in HFF, he concludes that in any modal group, (a) and (b) occur on the same notes irrespective of modal character: that is, in the Banjiki modal group, irrespective of whether a piece is in a Dorian mode (final B), Aeolian mode (final F$^\sharp$), or Lydian mode (final D), the notes on which (a) and (b) occur most frequently are A, D, E; in the Ōjiki modal group, (a) and (b) occur most frequently on G, C, D, irrespective of whether the mode is Dorian (final A) or Aeolian (final E); in the Sui modal group, (a) and (b) occur most frequently on the notes G, D, A; in the Sō modal group, on the notes C, F, D; and in the Kaku modal group, on the notes A, D. A survey of the pieces in Systems I and II confirms Hayashi's conclusions (see later) for the group of pieces under consideration here. A few pieces in the Ōjiki and Sui modal groups do not conform to the general pattern, but these will be dealt with in a later study.[65]

The fact that the notes on which (a) and (b) occur is determined by key, rather than mode, may be significant in determining the meaning of these signs. In each modal group, the two notes on which (a) and (b) occur most frequently are the two degrees (in the series of notes common to all pieces in that group —

---

60   以 指 磨 穴

61   先 由 後 引

62   吹 舒 後 由 也

63   動 指

64   Hayashi, K. op.cit., pp.298-300.

65   See Marett, op.cit. (see n.2), Chapter III.

irrespective of final), that are separated from their lower neighbours by a semitone. Thus, in the Banjiki modal group: B C♯ [D] E F♯ G♯ [A]; in the Kaku modal group: F♯ G♯ [A] B C♯ [D] E; in the Ōjiki modal group; A B [C♯] D E F♯ [G]; in the Sui modal group: A B G♯ [D] E F♯ [G]; in the Sō modal group: G A B [C] D E [F]. The fact that (a) and (b) fall frequently on F♮ in the Sō mode, that is, a note separated by a semitone from its lower

neighbour, confirms that 五 yields F♮ , rather than F♯ , in this mode (see

p. 8). The significance of these data will be explained shortly.

First, let us consider the definition of (a) in the 'Notes on the Method of Scoring' (see p.10) namely, 'rub the hole with the finger'. While this definition does not specify which hole is to be rubbed, we might reasonably suppose that the hole referred to is the hole of the same name as the tablature-sign affected by (a), that is, in most fingerings,[66] the hole distal to the most distal stopped hole. The musical result of passing the finger-tip back and forth across this hole is a lowering and raising of the pitch of the note, that is, a mordent. Since it is unlikely that complete closure of the hole results from rubbing, the mordent probably covered a semitone only. The observation (see preceding paragraph) that (a) occurs most frequently on the two notes of the scale separated from their *lower* neighbours by just such an interval, supports the suggestion that it is the neighbouring, open, distal hole that is to be rubbed. This interpretation of (a) is further supported by the fact that (a) and (b) *never* affect the

tablature-sign 口 (all holes closed). In this fingering, there is no open distal

hole, or indeed, *any* open hole, available to be rubbed.

The definition of (a) (rub the finger-hole) does not indicate the rhythm in which the ornament is to be performed. The definitions of (b), 'first (a); afterwards prolong' and of (c) 'prolong by blowing; afterwards (a)' are, on the other hand, instructions with rhythmical implications. The symbols by which (b) and (c) are notated (see p. 10), may give a clue to their *specific* rhythm. In each case, the notation consists of four signs: three are prolongation signs[67], one is (a). Since in most instances (b) affects tablature-signs with a duration of one beat (see p.18), it is likely that each of the four component signs of (b) represent a quarter of a beat. Similarly, each component sign of (c) might represent a quarter of a beat. In view of this, the meanings suggested by the notation of (b) and (c) are: for (b), 'execute a mordent (a) in the first quarter of the beat'; for (c), 'execute a mordent (a) in the final quarter of the beat'.

Of the two signs, ((a), (b)) that occur in the notation, only one, namely (b) is clearly and rhythmically defined: the definition of (a) does not give any

---

[66] In the 六 fingering only, (a) is executed by rubbing the finger-hole *above* the most

proximal finger-hole, that is 六 [VII] (the only hole open in this fingering, see p. 3).

[67] The sign 引 ; (see p. 13).

11

rhythmical details — it merely instructs the performer *what* to do, not *when* to do it. Although (c) does not occur in the notation it is, like (b), clearly and rhythmically defined. In short, (a) is given rhythmical characterization only in the definitions of (b) and (c), and is of little use as a musical sign in itself. Why then, does (a) rather than (c) occur in the notations? A possible explanation is, that because of the complexity of the signs (b) and (c), one of them, namely, (c) was abbreviated by dropping the three prolongation signs from the notation: (c) would then be written as (a), and (b) as before (that is with three prolongation signs). The fact that (a) is the more frequent of the two signs ((a), (b)) supports the suggestion that it is an abbreviation for the more frequent of the more complex pair ((b), (c)), namely, (c). Accordingly, (a) has been interpreted as a delayed mordent and (b) as a mordent. It is unlikely that the ornament was executed precisely within a quarter of a beat as the notation suggests. It is more likely that (a) indicates that a mordent is to be executed *as near as possible to the end of the note,* and (b) indicates that a mordent is to be executed, like the western mordent, *as near as possible to the beginning of the note.* The notation of (a) and (b) is the most accurate representation of these concepts possible with the signs used in HFF.

Because of its similarity to the western mordent, (b) has been transcribed

✲ . A new notational convention has been adopted for (a), namely, ✲ . The

effect of (b) in performance is quite different from that of (a). (b) is a mordent; (a) has the effect of an anacrusis to the succeeding beat.

METRE AND MENSURAL NOTATION

The remaining signs defined in the section of HFF headed 'Notes on the Method of Scoring': are as follows:

'The lexigraph — (ichi); interrupt the breath[68]'.

' 丿 [= 弓〕] (hiku): lengthen by long blowing; (the cursive character)[69]'.

' 火 (ka): very quickly[70]'.

68   一 字 絶 氣

69   長 吹 舒 也 行 字 也

70   火 急

' 百 (hyaku)[71]: when 百 is beside [the tablature-sign], the taiko[72] [is to be struck] [73] '.

'Red dots beside the character: blow the breath in[74] '.

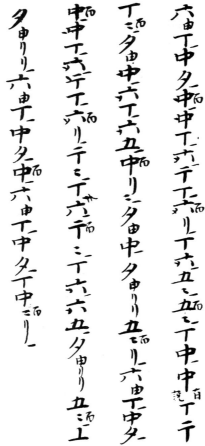

Figure 2: 'The Waves of Kokonor' (A60a, 60b). Reproduction from microfilm

[71] This may be a substitute for 拍 meaning 'to strike with the hand'. In Chinese of the Tang period, the sounds for 百 and 拍 were respectively *pɐk* and *p'ɐk*

(B. Karlgren, *Grammata Serica Recensa* 781a, 782m). (Picken, L.E.R., 'Tenri Toshokan shozō no jūyō na Tōgaku-fu ni kansuru oboegaki' in *Biblia*, Vol.57 (1974).

[72] 太 鼓 . The bass drum.

[73] 百 旁 即 太 鼓 也

[74] 字 邊 朱 點 氣 吹 入 也

13

' 丁 (tei): small pause; old scores use it[75] '.

The last sign listed, namely tei, does not occur in HFF and will not be discussed here. Red dots beside the note signify over-blowing (see p. 27) and are not relevant to the topic of this section.

In order to establish the precise significance of the remaining four signs, their function in two pieces, 'The Waves of Kokonor'[76] and 'Liquidamber Incense (Entering Broaching)[77]' will be considered in detail. Figure 2 is the notation of 'The Waves of Kokonor' as it appears on folios 60a, 60b of Copy A. A transcription of this piece appears on p. 55.

The drum-beat sign 百 occurs 12 times, at intervals, to the right of certain tablature-signs in the columns of notation (read from top to bottom and from right to left). It may be postulated that the main drum-beat will fall at regular intervals throughout the piece, and that twelve periods, in binary or quarternary metre (since irregular or ternary metres are rare in Chinese and Sino-Japanese music[78]), will be defined by these drum-beats.

In the following discussion, specific mensural values (based on definitions given in HFF) will be proposed for each of the signs in Figure 2. It will be shown that, with all these values taken into account, the notation yields twelve bars in regular metre.

As a preliminary hypothesis, let us suppose that each tablature-sign (see p. 3) occupies one time-unit — one beat — in execution. In this piece there are 66 tablature-signs. The maximum number of tablature-signs between drum-beats is seven[79] and the minimum, four.[80] If the metre is indeed binary or some multiple of this, then certain notes must last for more than, or less than, one unit of duration. In the 'Notes on the Method of Scoring', the sign 引 is defined as 'lengthen by long blowing'. We might assume that this sign lengthens the preceding note by one beat. Further, the sign 二 (two, twice), cursively written as two dots, also occurs in the manuscript, but is not defined in the 'Notes'. In its cursive form, the sign 二 is used in Chinese texts to indicate a

75 小息古譜用也

76 青海波

77 蘇合香入破

78 Picken, L.E.R., 'Secular Chinese Songs of the Twelfth Century' *Studia Musicologica Academiae Scientiarum Hungaricae, VIII* (1966), p.134.

79 In periods beginning on the third, ninth, and eleventh, drum-beats in Figure 2.

80 In periods beginning on the second, sixth, and eighth, drum-beats in Figure 2.

repetition of the preceding lexigraph; in a musical notation, therefore, it might mean repetition of the preceding tablature-sign. Musical Example 1 is a transcription of the notation in Figure 2 using the values proposed up to this point. A note followed by $\mathcal{J}|$ is transcribed as a minim. (A list of all signs used in transcription and their equivalents in the notation of HFF appears on p. 26).

Musical Example 1

If the effect of the $\mathcal{J}|$ and $\backsim$ signs is taken into consideration, the total number of beats rises to 80; the maximum number of observed beats in a drum-beat period becomes eight[81]; and the minimum is now six.[82]

In the light of this result, it seems probable that the 12 drum-beats define measures of eight beats, and that some hitherto unrecognized duration sign is operative in those measures that are deficient in beats. A sign not so far taken into consideration is $\frown$ (transcribed as |). Although merely defined as 'interrupt the breath', $\frown$ punctuates the text in such a way as to suggest that it has a *metrical* function. In Figure 2 groups consisting of varying numbers of tablature-signs occur between $\frown$ signs as follows:

5 groups of one sign
26 groups of two signs
2 groups of three signs
3 groups of five signs

Groups of two signs are thus very much more frequent than other groups. This observation, coupled with the fact that the largest number of $\frown$ in a single drum-beat period is four, suggests that an eight-beat measure was conceived as subdivided into groups of two tablature-signs (beats), or groups of whole-number multiples of two. If, therefore, $\frown$ defines binary groups (or multiples thereof), non-binary groups, consisting of an odd number of beats, must be

---

[81]   In periods beginning on the third and ninth drum-beats in Musical Example 1.

[82]   In periods beginning on the second, sixth and eighth drum-beats in Musical Example 1.

15

supplemented in some way to yield an even number of beats. The simplest way to achieve this is to prolong the last note of an odd-numbered group by one beat. This would not present any difficulty to a performer reading, for the first time, a part such as that reproduced in Figure 2.

Musical Example 2 is a transcription of the notation in Figure 2 in which the sign ⌣ is given the value postulated above. Where the last note of an odd-numbered group is prolonged, the note that represents the extra beat is marked with a cross (+) and tied to the preceding beat, thus ♩♪♯ (see p. 27).

Musical Example 2

The notation of 'The Waves of Kokonor', thus yields 64 beats in binary groups, made up as follows:

26 groups of 2 beats (52 beats in all)
3 groups of 4 beats (12 beats in all)

To each of the groups containing an odd number of beats, we have added one beat as follows:

5 groups of 1 beat (plus 5 beats, one for each group, yields 10 beats in all)
2 groups of 3 beats (plus 2 beats, one for each group, yields 8 beats in all)
1 group of 5 beats (plus 1 beat, yields 6 beats in all).

The total number of beats accounted for by the groups of odd numbers of beats is 24 (=10+8+6). This sum, added to the total number of beats in groups of even numbers of beats (64), yields a total of 88 for the entire piece. This total is only eight beats short of the total expected for 12 eight-bar measures. Is there any remaining feature of the tablature not so far examined, which might account for the missing eight beats? A peculiarity of this notation is the use of two different signs to indicate prolongation, namely 𝟹| and ⌣ . The definition of ⌣ as an articulation sign: 'interrupt the breath', limits its usefulness in prolonging a note to those places where the note to be prolonged is followed by a break — perhaps produced by tonguing. The sign 𝟹| without a following ⌣ may be interpreted as a prolongation-sign without a following

16

break, as (for example) in bars 14 and 15 of the transcription of 'The Peaceful City' (p. 35).

An underlying limitation of the rhythmic notation postulated up to this point is the lack of indication for prolongation in excess of two beats. Since a prolongation of two beats followed by a break is indicated by a single tablature-sign and ⌣ , while a prolongation of two beats *without* a following break is indicated by a note followed by 𝄍| alone, a prolongation of four beats might be indicated, with plausible economy of signs, by 𝄍| followed by

⌣ . This would take advantage of the established function of ⌣ as an indicator of a note prolonged to twice its length, and would be unambiguous.

Musical Example 3 is a transcription of 'The Waves of Kokonor' (Figure 2) in which this interpretation of 𝄍| ⌣ is followed.

Musical Example 3

As seen in Musical Example 3, there are four notes prolonged (transcribed as ♩⌣♩) by 𝄍| and followed by ⌣ . The total durational value of these four notes is thus increased from 8 to 16 beats. In this manner the eight beats required to fill out the 12 measures of eight beats (96 beats in all) are supplied. The postulated structure is now complete. A fully edited transcription of 'The Waves of Kokonor' appears on p. 55.

Further examination of all instances in pieces in Systems I and II where a tablature-sign is followed by 𝄍| ⌣ shows that, in practice prolongation is implied only when 𝄍| ⌣ follows the first or fifth beat, and not when it follows beats 3 or 6. (see p.18). Observation has shown that notes are never prolonged across bars or half-bars.

17

The prolongation of the final beat of a group consisting of an odd number of beats, so as to fill out a binary or quarternary structure, has a precedent in the Chinese setting of seven-syllable lines (one note to one syllable) to eight-beat musical measures. Picken[83] suggests, 'that a line of seven monosyllabic words was normally sung to seven notes in a measure of eight units, the seventh word and note — *and a breath, if required* (my emphasis) — occupying the last two of these eight units.' Two of the most popular forms of song-texts in Tang China (whence all tunes transcribed in this paper were imported to Japan) were exclusively seven-syllable-line forms, such as the quatrain *jueju* and the seven-syllable *lüshi*.[84] This aspect of the mensural notation may, therefore, be related to a general principle in Tang musical practice. It is to be noted that, in 8/4 measures, in 'The Waves of Kokonor' and other Tang-music pieces the regulating drum-beat falls not on the first beat of the measure (as in western music), but on the fifth beat. Summarizing the results so far, it may be concluded that:

(i)   each unqualified tablature-sign represents a note of one beat duration;

(ii)   二 placed after a note indicates that the note is to be repeated;

(iii)   ⌒ marks the end of a group of signs equivalent to an even number of beats; where ⌒ terminates a group of an odd number of signs the last note is to be prolonged by one beat;

(iv)   a note followed by 引 is to be sustained for two beats; when

followed, on beats two or six of any measure, by ⌒ , thus, 引 ⌒ , it is to be sustained for four beats.

One more example must be considered. Figure 3 is the notation of 'Liquidamber Incense (Entering Broaching)' as it appears on folio 50a of Copy A. A transcription of this appears on p. 45.

In addition to the signs used in 'The Waves of Kokonor', this piece

includes the sign 火 . Defined as 'very quickly', this sign is interpreted as

halving the duration of a note (that is, as the converse of 引).

In a regular measured structure, such as that of 'The Waves of Kokonor', with strictly binary ratios between note values, a measure is unlikely to include a single half-beat note. In order to complete a single beat in such a structure, a second half-beat note is required; such notes are likely to occur in pairs. Only seven instances of two consecutive tablature-signs, each followed by 火 , occur

[83]   Picken, op.cit. (1966), p.131.

[84]   Liu, James, J.G., The Art of Chinese Poetry (London, 1962), pp.26-29.

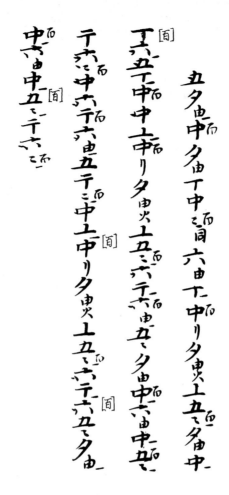

Figure 3: 'Liquidamber Incense' (A50a). Reproduction from microfilm

in pieces in System I,[85] and four[86] in pieces in System II, however. The necessity for a second half-beat note to complete a beat, once the first half-beat note has been indicated, makes the notation of a second 火 unnecessary. Consequently, in 85 instances in System I, 火 occurs only after the first sign in the notation of a pair of quavers, almost certainly as an abbreviation of the fuller notation. System II displays the long-hand notation for a pair of quavers (that is with two

---

[85]   In 'Samajja' (4): 'The Peaceful City' (1); 'Humming and Ball Games' (1); 'The Floating Dragon-Boats' (1).

[86]   In 'Lengthening Summer' (3); 'Long Life' (1).

火) more often (four times) than the abbreviated version (three times)[87]. Five instances[88] where 火 follows the *second* of a pair of quavers in pieces in System I, result perhaps from the omission of the first 火 from the long-hand notation.

A different convention is adopted for the abbreviated notation of *four* consecutive quavers (System I only). For example, the following passage, where four successive quavers are implied, occurs twice in 'The Juggling Pavilion':

中 夕 由 火 五 上 火 ｜ . In the first variant (from Sadayasu's score)

that follows this piece (see p.36), this passage is notated as follows:

中火 夕火 五火 上火 ｜ ', that is, with a 火 following each

tablature-sign. It appears that the former notation (with only two 火) is an abbreviation of the latter notation (with four 火). The latter notation also occurs in 'Respect for Wisdom' (three times), and the former in 'Joyful Spring' (twice)[89]. In 'The Floating Dragon-Boats (Entering Broaching)' (four instances), the notation is abbreviated further so that the 火 occurs only after the second

tablature sign, thus: 中 六 火 テ Ｔ ｜ .

Where a tablature-sign followed by 火 is, in turn, succeeded by ⌒ :

中 火 ｜ ('Taking up the Zither', b.11), or 六 火 ｜ ('Sword

Vapours (Kodatsu)', bar 14), it is read in the rhythm ♩ ７ ｜ .

A total of 16 drum-beats is shown in Figure 3. Ryūmeishō[90] states, however, that there should be 20 drum-beats in this piece and, in the Figure, missing drum-beat signs have been added in brackets, in the light of the following discussion.

Without taking into account the additional beats suggested by the sign ⌒ , the total number of beats is 70. When the rhythmical and metrical effects of ⌒ are taken into account (as in the analysis of 'The Waves of Kokonor') there are:

12 groups of 2 beats (24 beats in all)
2 groups of 4 beats (8 beats in all)

---

[87] In 'The Well of the Nettletree-Leaf' (1); 'Huangdi' (1); 'Miss Cao (Stamping-dance)' (1).

[88] In 'Joyful Spring' (3); 'Great Radiance' (1); 'The Autumn Wind' (1).

[89] 夕 上 由 火 五 上 火 In bar 3 of 'Joyful Spring' the first 火 sign has

been omitted in error.

[90] GSRJ, XIX, p.53.

In all, then, there are 32 beats in binary groupings. In addition there are the following non-binary groups:

2 groups of 1 beat (plus 2 beats, one for each group, yields 4 beats in all)
3 groups of 3 beats (plus 3 beats, one for each group, yields 12 beats in all)
4 groups of 5 beats (plus 4 beats, one for each group, yields 24 beats in all)
1 group of 7 beats (plus 1 beat, yields 8 beats in all).

The number of beats implicit in non-binary groupings is thus 48. In all, this yields 80 beats (32+48), or 20 measures of four beats.[91] In the four-beat measures of this piece, the drum-beat falls on the third beat. Most measured movements in Systems I and II are in either 8/4 (百 　 on beat 5) like 'The Waves of Kokonor', or 4/4 (百 　 on beat 3) like 'Liquidamber Incense (Entering Broaching)'. A number of movements (including both Kodatsu) are in more than one metre, however: 'Sword Vapours (Kodatsu)' (see p. 52) includes measures in 6/4 (百 　 on beat 5) and 4/4 (百 　 on beat 3); 'Miss Cao (Broaching, Kodatsu)' is in 8/4 (百 　 on beat 7) and 4/4 (百 　 on beat 3); 'Miss Cao (Stamping-dance)' is in 6/4 (百 　 on beat 5) and 8/4 (百 　 on beat 7) (see p. 59). A transcription of 'Liquidamber Incense (Entering Broaching)' appears on p. 45.

In view of the strong evidence presented above for the interpretation of 一 as a metrical sign, it is not immediately clear why the sign is defined as a phrase-mark ('interrupt the breath'), rather than as a metrical indicator. A possible reason for adopting this definition is, however, that while 一 functions as a phrasing indicator in *all* movements in Systems I and II, it is a metrical indicator in measured movements only; in unmeasured movements (Preludes[92]) it has no metrical significance at all. Further study of HFF (the results of which will appear in a future publication) has shown that where 一 acts as a prolongation-sign, after odd-numbered beats, and after a tablature-sign followed by 引 , the metre is characterized as 'mabyōshi'[93]. The existence of a term to denote the metrical usage of 一 supports the view that a function

---

[91] There are errors in the notation of this piece (see p.45), but these do not affect the total number of beats.

[92] *Jo* 序

[93] 間 拍 子

21

such as that deduced in the preceding analysis was indeed attributed to the sign in Heian musical notation.

The transcriptions of measured movements in Systems I and II (pp.27-59) have been compared with versions in later 'Tang-music' sources, namely, the early fourteenth century mouth-organ score, Shinsen shōteki-fu (SSSTF) (1302), JCYR and SGYR. Where errors in the notation of HFF have been revealed, transcriptions have been emended. All emendations, together with the name of the Tang-music score in which the correct version occurs, are noted below each transcription.

In all, 199 emendations have been made: on average, about one emendation to every three measures. It is important to bear in mind that the manuscript under discussion is a late copy of a tenth-century source, the mensural notation of which was probably unintelligible to musicians and copyists after the end of the Heian period (1185); in such circumstances complete accuracy cannot be expected. The number of emendations required is not in excess of that which might be made necessary by copyists' errors, nor has any one sign been supplied or deleted in numbers that might suggest that the interpretation offered is incorrect. The strongest evidence in favour of the values for signs in HFF suggested in this paper is, however, the music itself: such regular and musically satisfactory melodies are unlikely to have emerged if the interpretation of the notation were wrong in any major respect.

TITLES IN HFF

In the following list of titles in HFF, only titles of pieces of which all, or part, has been transcribed are translated. The translations are, at present, tentative. Titles in brackets are those, listed in the Table of Contents of the manuscript, for which no notation occurs in the body of the manuscript. Each title is preceded by its folio number in Copy A (numbering through from the beginning of Volume I to the end of Volume II).

Sō-jō kyoku	雙 調 曲	*Pieces in the Sō Mode*	
5b	Ryūka-en	柳 花 菀	Willow-Flower Garden
6a	Shunteiraku	春 庭 樂	The Spring Palace
6b	Yuki tsukuri-mono	悠 紀 作 物	
7a	Suki tsukurimono	主 基 作 物	

Ōjiki-chō kyoku 黃 鐘 調 曲   *Pieces in the Ōjiki Mode*

7b	Sekihatsu tōrika *or* Sekihaku tōrika	赤 白 桃 李 花	Pink and White Peach and Plum Blossoms
9b	Kishunraku	喜 春 樂	Joyful Spring

22

11a	Saibara	催 馬 樂	Saibara[94]
12a	Chōseiraku	長 生 樂	Long Life
13a	Saiōraku	西 王 樂	The Queen of the Western Paradise
13b	Kainraku	夏 引 樂	Lengthening Summer
14b	Kayōsei	榎 葉 井	The Well of the Nettletree-Leaf (*Celtis sinensis*)
15a	Ōtenraku	應 天 樂	Obeying the Will of Heaven
15b	Seijōraku	清 上 樂	Seijō[95]
16b	Kanzeiraku	感 城 樂	The Thankful City
17a	Anzeiraku	安 城 樂	The Peaceful City
17b	Rōdenraku	弄 殿 樂	The Juggling Pavilion
18a	Kanampo	河 南 浦	Honan Riverbank
18b	Kaiseiraku	海 青 樂	The Sea is Blue
19a	Yōgūraku	央 宮 樂	The Central Palace
	(Eiyūraku)	英 雄 樂	
19b	Ōdai-Santai	皇 帝 三 臺	Huangdi[96]
20a	Sangin-Tagyūraku	散 吟 打 球 樂	Humming and Ball-games[97]

[94] Saibara is the name of a Japanese Court-Music genre based on native folksong. The rubric 'Saibara' may here be a heading, and not the title of the piece that succeeds it. Three of the succeeding pieces, 'Long Life', 'The Queen of the Western Paradise', 'Lengthening Summer', are listed under the heading 'Saibara' in Gakkaroku (NKZ, p.146).

[95] This piece is named after Ōto no Kiyogami (Seijō) 大 戸 清 上 (Gakkaroku, NKZ, p.944), a Japanese flute-master of the early ninth century.

[96] The Yellow Emperor, legendary first ruler of China. Santai 三 臺 literally, 'Three Towers' was a type of drinking song, popular in the Tang dynasty.

[97] This piece may be from the Sangaku genre. 'Chinese popular music, likewise, had made its way into Japan. It was known under the name *sangaku*, and included music of all kinds. Interspersed between dance numbers and songs were acrobatic feats, juggling, and particularly pole-climbing...' (Harich-Schneider, op.cit., p.52).

21a	Teikinraku	提琴樂	Taking up the Zither
21a	Shōenraku	承燕樂	
	(Tenanraku)	天安樂	
Sui-chō kyoku		水調曲	*Pieces in the Sui Mode*
21b	Hanryūshū	汎龍舟	The Floating Dragon-Boats
24a	Kyūjōraku	九城樂	The Nine Cities
25b	Jussuiraku	拾翠樂	Gathering Kingfishers
26a	Jūkōraku	重光樂	Great Radiance
	(Shōjunraku)	承淳樂	
Banjiki-chō kyoku		盤涉調曲	*Pieces in the Banjiki Mode*
26b	Genka	元哥	
31a	Banjiki Sangun	盤涉參軍	
39a	Agirō	阿娚娘	
43a	Taizoku-kaku-banjiki-chō	太簇角盤涉	
	Chōka-manzairaku	調鳥歌萬歲樂	
44b	Sokō	蘇合香	Liquidamber Incense
51a	Manjūraku	萬秋樂	Ten Thousand Autumns
54b	Sōmeiraku[98]	崇明樂	Respect for Wisdom
56a	Somakusha	蘇莫者	Samajja[99]
56b	Kenki-kodatsu	斂氣襌脫	Sword Vapours[100]

[98] In all copies the first character is 宗 . The correct form of the character is 崇 .

[99] Eckardt, op.cit., p.163.

[100] This title may derive from a Taoist story in which purple vapours in the sky indicated the presence of two buried swords. (Fukunaga, M. 'Taoists and Pre-taoists appearing on Mirrors and Swords' in *Tōyō Gakuhō 45* (Kyōto 1973) p.97). *Kodatsu* was a lively dance of Mongolian origin which took its name from a black hat of lamb-skin worn during the dance (Eckardt, op.cit., p.162).

57b	Shūfūraku	秋風樂		The Autumn Wind
58b	Chōkōraku	鳥向樂		Facing the Bird[101]
59b	Rindai	輪臺		Bügür[102]
60a	Seigai-ha	青海波		The Waves of Kokonor
60b	Saisōrō	採桑老		The Old Man Plucks Mulberry Leaves
60b	Chikurinraku	竹林樂		The Bamboo Grove
61a	Hakuchū	白柱		The White Pillar
61b	Shōshūraku	承秋樂		Continuing Autumn
61b	Kanshūraku	感秋樂		Moved by Autumn
62a	Tokubanji	德伴字		
62b	Yūjijo[103]	遊字女		Childrens' Games
Kaku-chō kyoku		角調曲		*Pieces in the Kaku Mode*
63a	Sōrō-kodatsu	曹娘禪脱		Miss Cao[104]
Ranjō		亂聲		
64a	Shingaku-ranjō	新樂亂聲		
65a	Rinyū-ranjō	林邑亂聲		
Rinyū		林邑		*Cambodian Music*
(Rinyū-ranjō)		林邑亂聲		
(Bosatsu)		菩薩薩		
(Michiyuki)		道行		

---

[101] Eckardt, op.cit., p.385.

[102] Eckardt, op.cit., p.173.

[103] The first character is written 逝 in all copies of HFF. The correct form is 遊 .

[104] *Kodatsu* See n.102.

(Tori)	鳥		
(Bairo)	倍	臚	
(Batō)	拔	頭	
Gigaku	伎	樂	
(Shishi)	師	子	
(Go-kō)	吳	公	
(Kongō)	金	剛	
(Karura)	迦	樓	羅
(Konron)	崑	崙	
(Rikishi)	力	士	
(Baromon)	婆	羅	門
(Daikoji)	大	狐	兒
(Suiko)	醉	胡	

TRANSCRIPTIONS OF MEASURED MOVEMENTS IN SYSTEMS I AND II

The meanings of the signs used in the transcriptions are as follows:

丨 = 一 (ichi) (see p. 15).

(丨) = an 一 has been ignored.

[丨] = an 一 has been supplied.

火 = 火 (ka) (see p. 18).

(火) = a 火 has been ignored.

[火] = a 火 has been supplied.

♩ = the tablature sign is followed by 引 .

(引) = a 引 has been ignored.

[引] = a 引 has been supplied.

$\bigg|^{+\,\big|}_{}$ = a note prolonged by ⌒ .

= a note prolonged by 弓) and followed by ⌒ .

○ = a red dot beside the tablature sign (over blowing).

Names of movements not transcribed are enclosed in square brackets in the heading to each Musical Example (see p.28). Comments that occur after titles in the manuscript are translated.

PIECES IN THE SŌ MODE

Willow-flower Garden: 20 drum-beats*. There is a song-text. New music.

Musical Example 4

1. The sign 火 is miswritten as a small 六 .

2. The signs 中 引 六 二 六 引 (b, d, d, d) are omitted in all copies (JCYR).

3. The instruction 'repeat what precedes 以 上 兩 反 ' occurs here.

27

4. The tablature sign 夕 (*a*) is duplicated in error in all copies.

*There are 24 drum-beats (= measures). The lexigraph 囬 (four) has been omitted.

The Spring Palace: 10 drum-beats. Old music.

Musical Example 5

1. The comment, 'there are two versions 有二説 ', occurs at this point.

PIECES IN THE ŌJIKI MODE

Pink and White Peach and Plum Blossoms ([Prelude], Broaching)

Musical Example 6

1. The sign ⌐ is omitted in Copy A, but not in B and C.
2. The sign ⌐ occurs in Copy A only, and has not been transcribed.
3. The comment, 'there are two versions', occurs at this point.
4. The tablature signs 六 中 (*d, b*) are omitted in all copies (JCYR, SSSTF).
5. The following instruction occurs here: '*Section IV*: now repeat Section II 四帖即以二帖反吹 .'

6. The tablature sign T (*c*) is omitted in Copy A, but not in B and C.

Joyful Spring ([Prelude], Entering Broaching)

Musical Example 7

1.   The comment, 'there are two versions', occurs at this point.

2.   The tablature signs ⊥ *9* (**g, a**) are substituted in all copies in

     place of the correct sign T (**c**). (JCYR, SSSTF)

3.   The sign ⌣ is omitted in Copy A, but not in B and C.

Long Life ([Prelude], Broaching) Prelude: 6 drum-beats; Broaching: 10 drum-beats*.

Musical Example 8

1. The sign 中 (*b*) is omitted in all copies (see bar 7).

* The movement is written out twice (with an altered beginning); there are therefore 20 drum-beats.

The Queen of the Western Paradise ([Prelude], Broaching)[1] Prelude: 7 drum-beats; Broaching: 10 drum-beats.

Musical Example 9

1.   There are many errors in the notation of this piece, particularly in the omission of tablature-signs. In making the above transcription, reference has been made to JCYR and SSSTF.

2.   The signs 丁 彐丨 (*e*) are omitted in all copies (see bar 9).

3.   The sign 丁 (*e*) is omitted in all copies (JCYR, SSSTF).

4.   The signs 丁 彐丨 (*e*) (or 丁丨) are omitted in all copies (JCYR, SSSTF).

5.   The sign 中 (*b*) is omitted in all copies (JCYR, SSSTF).

6.   The sign 丁 (*e*) is omitted in all copies (JCYR, SSSTF).

Lengthening Summer ([Prelude], Broaching) Prelude: 23   drum-beats; Broaching: 12 drum-beats.

Musical Example 10

1.   The sign 丄 (*g*) is omitted in all copies (see bars 2, 5).

The Well of the Nettletree-Leaf: 9 drum-beats.

Musical Example 11

32

1. The sign — occurs in Copies A and C, but not in Copy B. B is accepted.

Obeying the Will of Heaven: 20 drum-beats. New music.

Musical Example 12

1. The comment, 'there are two readings', occurs at this point.

2. The signs ⊥ 五 (*g*, *f♯*) are duplicated in error in all copies.

3. The sign — occurs in Copy A only and has not been transcribed.

Seijō: 20 drum-beats.
Musical Example 13

1. The signs 五 夕 引 (*f#*, *a*) are duplicated in error in all copies.
2. The signs 六 中 (*d*, *b*) are interpolated in error in all copies.

   They are not transcribed.

The Thankful City: 18 drum-beats. New music.

Musical Example 14

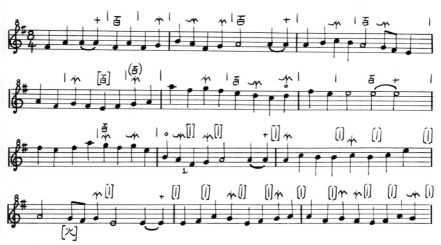

1. All 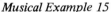 and 百 signs, and all red dots, are omitted in all copies from this point on. ⌒ signs supplied in transcription correspond to intra-columnary dots in SSSTF.

2. The sign ⌒ is omitted in all copies (bars 2, 8).

The Peaceful City: 16 drum-beats. New music.

Musical Example 15

1. The sign 夕 (*a*) is omitted in all copies (JCYR, SSSTF).

2. The comment, 'there are two version', occurs at this point.

35

The Juggling Pavilion: 14 drum-beats. There is no dance. New music.

Musical Example 16

1. The sign 百 is wrongly placed on this note in Copy A, but not in B and C.
2. The sign ⌒ is omitted in Copies A and C, but not in B.

3. The signs 百 and ⌒ are misplaced in Copy A, but not in B and C.
4. The sign 百 is placed 2 beats early in Copies A and C. Only in Copy B is it correctly placed.

Musical Example 16a: Variants from Prince Sadayasu's score

5. These versions appear to be alternatives to bar 2.

Musical Example 16b: Variant from Prince Sadayasu's score

6. This version appears to be an alternative to bars 13, 14.

Musical Example 16c: Variant from Prince Sadayasu's score

7.   This version appears to be an alternative to bars 7, 8.

Musical Example 16d: Variant from Prince Sadayasu's score

8.   This version appears to be an alternative to bars 13, 14.

Honan River-bank: 16 drum-beats. Old music.

Musical Example 17

1.   The comment, 'there are two versions', occurs at this point.

2.   The instruction, 'repeat 雨 反 ' occurs here.

3.   The sign ⌒ is omitted in Copy A, but not in B and C.

The Sea is Blue: There is no dance. 10 drum-beats.

Musical Example 18

1. The comment, 'there are two versions', occurs at this point.

The Central Palace: 12 drum-beats. New music.

Musical Example 19

1. The comment, 'there are two versions', occurs at this point.

Huangdi: 16 drum-beats. There is no dance. New music.

Musical Example 20

1.   There are two beats missing in all copies (possibly due to the omission of ⌒) between the fifth and sixth 百 signs.

2.   There are four beats missing in all copies between the twelfth and thirteenth 百 signs.

Humming and Ball-games: There is no dance. 12 drum-beats. (Two versions)
Version I:

Musical Example 21

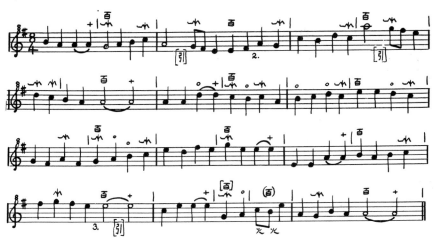

1. Following the first version of the tune in HFF is the comment 'this is a fine score 是 丰 譜 也 ,

2. The sign 五 ($f^\#$) is omitted in all copies (see Version II, bar 2).

3. The passage from the fifth beat of bar 9 does not agree with Version II, or with versions in later manuscripts.

Version II: 'the Master's version 師 説 ,

Musical Example 22

1. Version II differs from Version I at this point.

2. The signs 丁 由 中 (*c̄, b*) are duplicated in Copy A, but not in B and C.

3. Version II differs from Version I. The comment, 'there are two versions' occurs at this point.

4. The comment 'there are two versions', occurs at this point.

5. The sign ⌐ is omitted in Copies A and C, but not in B.

6. Two tablature-signs are missing in all copies. The notes supplied are tentative.

40

Taking up the Zither: 11 drum beats.

Musical Example 23

1.   The sign ⌢ is omitted in Copy A, but not in B and C.

PIECES IN THE SUI MODE

The Floating Dragon-Boats ([Prelude], Entering Broaching) There is no dance. Prelude: 16 drum-beats; Broaching: 18 drum-beats.

Musical Example 24

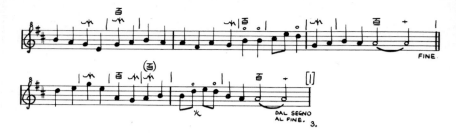

1. The sign ⌒ is misplaced in Copy A, but not in B and C.

2. The sign 同 'same', (what follows is the *same* as in the preceding Section) occurs in Copy B only.

3. The passage from the double bar is headed *Kantō* (exchange for the beginning) (see Picken, op.cit.1971, p.115). The sign 同 'same' (see n.2) occurs at the end of the passage.

The Nine Cities: There is no dance. Four Sections, each of which has 16 drum-beats. New Music.

Musical Example 25

43

1. The sign 火 appears to have been erroneously included in two instances (I, bars 2, 4).
2. In six instances the sign ⌐ implies prolongation for one beat where from a metrical point of view, there should be none.

3. The signs 丁 六 (c♯, d) are omitted in all copies (see III, bar 11).
4. The sign ⌐ is omitted in Copy A, but not in B and C.

5. The signs 中 六 由 (b, ã) are interpolated in all copies (I, bar 7).
6. The instruction 'Section IV: repeat the preceding Section' occurs here.

Gathering Kingfishers ([Prelude], Broaching) Prelude: 7 drum-beats; Broaching: 10 drum-beats.

Musical Example 26

1. The signs ⹀ and ⌐ are omitted in all copies (SSSTF).

2. The sign ⹁ (a) is omitted in Copy A, but not in B and C.

3. The sign ⌐ is omitted in Copy A, but not in B and C.
4. The sign ⌣ occurs in Copy A only and is not transcribed.

Great Radiance: 16 drum-beats. There is no dance. New music.

Musical Example 27

1. The sign 六 (*d*) is omitted in all copies (JCYR, SSSTF).

2. The signs ー and 百 are misplaced in Copy A, but not in B and C.

PIECES IN THE BANJIKI MODE

Liquidamber Incense ([Prelude], Entering Broaching, [Stamping-dance, Quick])
Prelude: five Sections. [Sections I and II]: 20 drum-beats [each]: Sections III, IV, V: 22 drum-beats [each]: Broaching: 20 drum-beats; Stamping-dance: 20 drum-beats; Quick: 20 drum-beats.

Musical Example 28

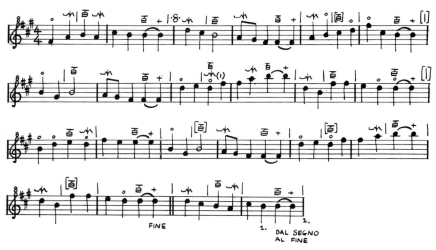

1. The sign 六 (*b*) is duplicated in error in all copies (SSSTF).

2. The sign 中 (*b*) is duplicated in error in all copies (SSSTF).

45

The passage from the double bar is headed *Kantō* ('exchange for the beginning'). The sign 同 , 'same' (what follows is the *same* as in the preceding Section) occurs at the end of the kantō, and at the point corresponding to the sign 𝄋 .

Ten Thousand Autumns ([Prelude], Broaching) Prelude: two Section: 18 drum-beats each; Broaching: six Sections: 18 drum-beats each.

Musical Example 29

47

1. The comment, 'there are two versions', occurs at this point.

2. All notes of this pitch are indicated by 口 . In this piece, each

   口 is followed by a 引| sign that appears to have no metrical significance.

3. The score reads 六 引|' 下 五 (♩ ♩ ♩). All later

   manuscripts consulted suggest that the reading in Section II, bar 5,

   namely, 六 下 五' (♩ ♩ ♩) is correct.

4. The sign ⌒ does not occur in this position in Sections II, III, IV, V.

5. The Section from the double bar, that is, the second half of the Section, is headed *Half-Section* 半 帖 .

6. The sign 同 'same' (what follows is the *same* as in the previous

   Section), occurs in Section II only, even though in other Sections the following passage is also the same.

7. The instruction, 'the Half Section is the same as in the preceding

   Section 半 帖 如 上 帖 ' occurs here.

8. The preceding three bars are omitted in Copy B and replaced by:

中 中 五 夕由 ┃ 中 夕由   *(b b ♭♯ d̂ b*

â).

9.   The sign ⊤ (*e*) is miswritten as ⊤ (*c♯*) in Copy A, but not in B and C.

10.   Section V differs from all other Sections at this point: where others

have 五 (*f♯*), Section V has 六 (*d*). The comment, 'there are

two versions' is written after the sign 六 .

11.   The instruction, 'the Half Section is the same as in the preceding Section' (see n.7) is omitted in all copies (JCYR, SSSTF).

12.   The comment, 'there are two versions' is written beside the sign 火 .

Respect for Wisdom ([Prelude], Entering Broaching) Prelude: 10 drum-beats. There is no dance. Broaching: 10 drum-beats. New music.

Musical Example 30

1.   The passage from the double bar is headed *Section II: Kantō*

(exchange for the beginning). The sign 同 'same' (what follows is

the *same* as in the preceding Section) occurs at a point corresponding to ·𝄋· in the transcription.

Samajja ([Prelude], [Entering] Broaching) [Prelude] : 6 drum-beats; Broaching:
12 drum-beats. Old music.

Musical Example 31

1. The sign 弓| does not occur in this position in the first variant
    version.
2. The sign ⊥ (g♯) is omitted in all copies (JCYR, SSSTF).
3. The passage from the double bar is headed *Section II: Kantō*

    (exchange for the beginning). The sign 同 , 'same' (what follows is

    the *same* as in the preceding Section) occurs at the end of the kantō,
    and at the point corresponding to the sign ·𝄋 .

Musical Example 31a: Variant from Prince Sadayasu's score

Musical Example 31b: another variant

4.   The signs  (g♯) are omitted in Copies A and C, but not in B.

Musical Example 31c: yet another variant

Musical Example 31d: a possible variant

5.   Red circles are superimposed on the tablature signs 夕 (*a*) 中
(*b*) 丁 (*c♯*) 六 (*d*) in Copies A and C.

Sword Vapours (Broaching, Kodatsu) Broaching: 20 drum-beats; Kodatsu: 16 drum-beats.
Broaching

Musical Example 32

1. The sign ⌒ is omitted in Copies A and C, but not in B.

2. The comment, 'there are two versions', occurs at this point.

3. The sign ⌒ is misplaced between the signs 丅 (e) and 六 (d) in Copy A, but not in B and C.

4. The instruction, 'repeat 兩 反 ' occurs here.

Kodatsu

Musical Example 33

1. The instruction, 'repeat 兩 反 ' occurs here.

2. A tablature-sign is missing after 夕火 : the identity of the sign is not known. The sign 五 has been supplied in transcription.

The Autumn Wind Five Sections: 16 beats each. But repeat Sections II and III, as Sections IV and V. New music.

Musical Example 34

Section II/Section IV 3.

Section III/Section V 3.

[2ᵈᵃ VOLTA AL FINE] 5.

1. The comment, 'there are two readings', occurs at this point.
2. The sign ⌣ is omitted in Copy A but not in B and C.
3. The following instruction occurs at the end of Section III: 'repeat Section II for Section IV; repeat Section III for Section V 四 帖

者 反 吹 二 帖 五 帖 者 反 吹 三 帖 ,

4. The passage from the double bar is headed *Section II*. The instruction *Kantō* (exchange for the beginning) has been omitted (see n.5). The sign 同 'same' (what follows is the *same* as in the preceding Section), miswritten here as 由 occurs in the manuscript at the point corresponding to the sign 𝄋.
5. The passage from the double bar is headed *Section III: Kantō* (see n.4). The sign 同 occurs at the end of this passage.

53

Facing the Bird Two Sections: 18 drum-beats each. There is no dance. New music.
Musical Example 35

1. The sign ⌣ is omitted in Copy A but not in B and C.
2. This section is headed *Half Section.*
3. The comment, 'there are two versions', occurs at this point.

Bügür: 16 drum-beats

Musical Example 36

The Waves of Kokonor: 12 drum-beats. New music.

Musical Example 37

1. The comment, 'there are two versions', occurs at this point.

2. The signs ⊥ 勹 由 (g♯ ⌢a) have been omitted in all copies

(see b.10) (JCYR, SSSTF).

3. The sign 六 (*d*) has been substituted for the correct sign 中 (*b*)

in all copies (JCYR, SSSTF).

The Old Man Plucks Mulberry Leaves: 12 drum-beats

Musical Example 38

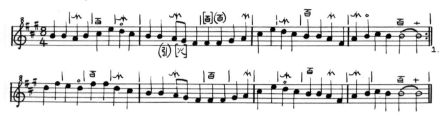

1. The instruction, 'repeat what precedes 以 上 兩 反 ,
    occurs here.

The Bamboo Grove: 10 drum-beats

Musical Example 39

1. The signs 五 (*f♯*) are omitted in Copies A and C. Only the sign

一 is omitted in Copy B.

The White Pillar: 8 drum-beats. There is no dance.

Musical Example 40

1. The comment, 'there are two versions', occurs here. Two versions of this piece are known. The version in HFF, (beginning on *a* and 8 bars in length) occurs also in SGYR, but as a second version; all other scores consulted have a nine-bar version that begins on *d*.
2. From this point to the end, HFF and the version in SGYR differ from all other versions.

Continuing Autumn: 10 drum-beats.

Musical Example 41

Moved by Autumn: 10 drum-beats.

Musical Example 42

1. The sign ⌒ is omitted in Copy A, but not in B and C.

2. The sign 有 is omitted in Copy A, but not in B and C.

Childrens' Games: 10 drum-beats.

Musical Example 43

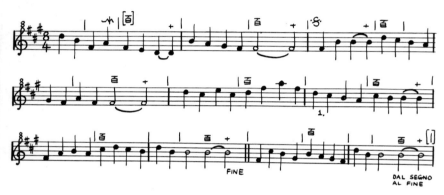

1. The sign 六 (*d*) is duplicated in error in all copies.

2. The passage from the double bar is headed: *Kantō* (exchange for the beginning) The sign 同 'same' (what follows is the *same* as in the preceding Section) occurs in the manuscript at the point corresponding to 𝄋 .

58

PIECES IN THE KAKU MODE

Miss Cao ([Prelude], Broaching, Kodatsu, Stamping-dance) Prelude: 7 drum-beats; Broaching: 6 drum-beats; Kodatsu: 8 drum-beats.

Broaching

Musical Example 44

Kodatsu

Musical Example 45

Stamping-dance

Musical Example 46

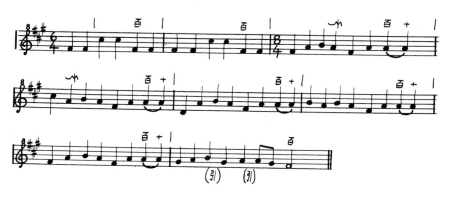

I am indebted to Dr. Picken for his assistance in the preparation of this paper, and to Dr. D.E. Mills, Mr. R. Somers, and Mr. T. Barrett, for advice regarding translations.

Trikāla:
A demonstration of augmentation and diminution from South India

D.R. WIDDESS

(Gonville and Caius College, Cambridge)

INTRODUCTION

Augmentation may be defined as the repetition of a rhythmic pattern at progressively slower speeds, that is to say with a proportional lengthening of the note-values at each repetition. The reverse process — speeding up of the pattern — is diminution. The relationship between the original and each new tempo is usually a simple mathematical ratio — 1:2, 1:4 or *vice versa* — and in polyphonic music, other parts may continue in the original tempo throughout.

The technique has long been known to Western musical theorists, if comparatively rarely used by composers. The Renaissance theory of proportions provided an appropriate system of notation, and augmentation and diminution are traditional ingredients of the art of academic fugue; but examples of the practical application of these theoretical developments are relatively few.[1] It is therefore of the greatest interest to find the technique in use in a non-European musical culture, indeed in a largely improvised art-form independent of musical notation. The short example of South Indian instrumental music transcribed below — called *Trikāla* — is a perfect demonstration of augmentation and diminution, in which the basic rhythmic pattern (*tāla*) appears, in all, at six different speeds.

The Trikāla forms the central episode of an extended improvisation[2] on *rāga* Śaṅkarābharaṇam, an Ionian mode with alternative flattened seventh, and *tāla* Miśra Cāpu, a rhythmic cycle of seven rapid beats. The instruments are flute,

---

[1] C. Sachs, *Rhythm and Tempo* (New York, 1953), p.238, notes examples of progressive diminution in a motet of Philippe de Vitry (1291-1361), two masses of Obrecht (c. 1450-1505), a mass (1503) by Brumel, and the *Missa "L'homme armé"* (c. 1570) of Palestrina. The seventh fugue of Bach's *Art of Fugue* is an exceptionally complex example of both augmentation and diminution. In the present century, the works of Elliott Carter (for example: String Quartet no. 1, 1951, last movement) and others show a renewed interest in techniques of this kind.

[2] Recorded on Nonesuch H-72052 side 1. Performers: T. Viswanathan (flute), L. Shankar (violin), T. Ranganathan (mṛdaṅgam). Sleeve notes by J.B. Higgins.

61

violin and mṛdaṅgam (a horizontal cylindrical drum with a "head" at each end, played with the fingers of both hands). The Trikāla is based on a short melodic theme, and is preceded and followed by sections of free improvisation on the same melody. The performance begins with an improvisation on the rāga by flute and violin, in free tempo without mṛdaṅgam accompaniment, and ends with an improvisation on the tāla by mṛdaṅgam alone. The overall form and style is called *Pallavi* — literally "tendril" or "creeping plant" — denoting in musical terminology an extended and elaborate fantasia in which the performers tax to the utmost their skill in melodic and rhythmic improvisation.[3]

One of the characteristic features of Pallavi-improvisation is the *trikāla* technique (Sanskrit *tri* = three, *kāla* = time), in which a basic melody is presented in a series of progressively quicker or slower tempi. As its name implies, only three levels of speed are normally involved: the original tempo, double or half tempo, and quadruple or quarter tempo. In the present example, the melody is heard first at its original tempo, then in *three* augmented versions: at half, a third and a quarter of the original speed. The introduction of the melody at a third of the speed is a remarkable extension of the traditional technique. Moreover, the augmentation process just described is then reversed, and by a corresponding process of diminution the melody appears once more at a third, half and finally at the original tempo. The succession of speeds is expressed in the transcription as a series of time-signatures (note-values remaining constant throughout):

$$\frac{7}{8} \qquad \frac{7}{4} \qquad \frac{7}{\text{♩.}} \qquad \frac{7}{2} \qquad \frac{7}{\text{♩.}} \qquad \frac{7}{4} \qquad \frac{7}{8}$$

In this way four principal levels of speed are used. However, the picture is complicated by the fact that the melodic theme itself embraces two distinct tempi, as we shall shortly see.

The changes of speed between repetitions of the melody are so precisely executed, without any break, that the original tempo can be regarded as continuing throughout, the whole augmentation-diminution process being an elaborate cross-rhythm against the basic tāla-pattern. This is audibly demonstrated by a fourth member of the ensemble (probably the tāmbūrā player, who also provides a continuous drone) who indicates, by hand-claps, the pattern of the tāla at its original tempo throughout the Trikāla. In so doing he not only provides a reference-point for the other musicians, but also introduces an element of rhythmic counterpoint, for during the augmentations and diminutions his claps frequently appear as syncopations.

The seven beats of the tāla Miśra Cāpu are customarily grouped 3 + 2 + 2:

[3] For a detailed discussion of Pallavi, see P. Sambamoorthy, *South Indian Music* (Madras 1954) vol. IV, pp.19-51.

In the present performance, the fourth and sixth beats are clapped (the first was probably indicated by a silent wave of the hand):

Hand-clap:

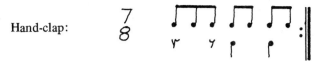

The melody itself begins on the second beat, and ends on the first; however, neither of these beats is stressed or clapped[4]. Clearly the modern Western concept of division into bars, with its attendant implications of "strong" and "weak" beats, has no relevance here: the distinction between beats is more one of function — clapped or unclapped, initial or final — than one of stress. For present purposes, however, time-signatures and some form of barring are desirable in order to make the structure of the piece clear to the reader. Since, in the present example, the melody begins on the *second* beat of the basic pattern (above), and since all tempo changes take effect from this same beat, it has been convenient to regard it as the *first* beat of a seven-beat bar, which then has the pattern 2 + 2 + 2 + 1:

Hand-clap:

In the transcription this internal structure is indicated by short bar-lines between the staves.

The melodic theme follows the traditional form, having two phrases (*A* and *B*) each of two bars' duration, separated by a rest. A repeat of the first phrase is necessary to complete the melody. At the beginning of the second, rhythmic part of the performance, the melody is sung by the flautist, solo, to Tamil words.

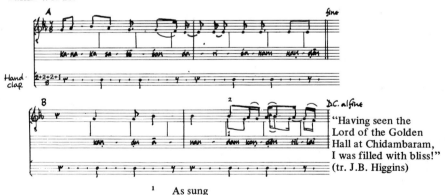

"Having seen the Lord of the Golden Hall at Chidambaram, I was filled with bliss!" (tr. J.B. Higgins)

[1] As sung
[2] Variant subsequently played on flute (violin plays 1)

[4] Later in the performance the first beat is also clapped, but more lightly than the fourth and sixth.

Here the first phrase (*A*) appears to be highly syncopated. However, it is better understood as employing the pattern of the tāla at a speed twice as fast as the basic tempo (which appears in *B*):

Thus the Trikāla is based on a melody which in itself combines two different tempi — a recognized feature of Pallavi melody reflecting the virtuoso character of this style-form.

In the Trikāla the rhythmic shape of the melody is preserved in all its transformations. The melody is first taken up at the beginning of phrase *B*, and phrases *B, A* and *B* played at the basic tempo. Each repetition of the melody thereafter comprises *A* and *B* only, after which *A* appears again at the next level of speed. An extra repetition of *A* completes the melody at the end. Taking into account the difference in tempo between phrases *A* and *B*, the structure of the piece may be represented as in Fig. 1 (the dotted line represents the constant speed of the tāla). In this way the present example of *trikāla* employs not three but six different tempi. A short cadenza on the mṛdaṅgam, in which the tāla pattern is elaborated at its quickest speed (7/16), brings this marvellous display of rhythmic virtuosity to a close.

While rhythmic manipulation constitutes the main interest of the Trikāla, melodic development is not entirely absent, for the augmented versions of the melody are not literal restatements. The note A♭, which appears six times as a passing-note in the original version of the melody, is almost entirely absent in the augmented variants, where it is confined to the ornamentation; G, B♭ and C are substituted for it. This may perhaps be explained in terms of the structure of the rāga[5]:

5 This analysis is based on the complete Pallavi performance.

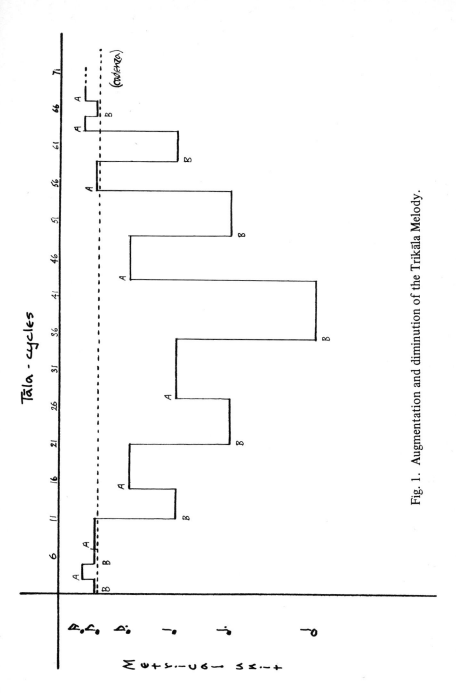

Fig. 1. Augmentation and diminution of the Trikāla Melody.

The rāga is essentially pentatonic, A♭ and D♭/♮ being unemphasised auxiliaries. The melody itself is even simpler in structure, emphasising the third-chain E♭ – G – B♭ (extended downwards in ornamentation to C). Prolongation of the A♭, by preserving it literally in the slower versions of the melody, would perhaps emphasize it to an extent out of keeping with the structure of the melody and of the rāga[6].

As a result, the augmented versions of the melody are also analytical simplifications, exposing both the rhythmic and the melodic structure of the melody. Similarly the ornamentation, though a little more elaborate in the slower versions, is slowed down, and becomes more audible. The effect is striking. From the opening section, where at a meteoric speed of 7/16-7/8 the complex rhythmic, melodic and ornamental schemes pass almost too quickly for the ear to grasp, we move gradually through slower versions, where all becomes temporarily clear, to the central section where the structure is almost too protracted for the mind to comprehend. This transformation is balanced by a return to the original speed during which the different tempi are more sharply contrasted (see Fig. 1). Finally, everything dissolves in the rapid cross-rhythms of the mr̥daṅgam cadenza. Meanwhile, the relationship between the tāla (represented by the hand-claps) and the melody constantly changes, but never resolves a fundamental rhythmic tension within the melody itself. This complex and dynamic process is a remarkable extension of traditional techniques, but one that is entirely at one with the time-honoured principles of Hindu art. The concept of *multum ex uno* is of course fundamental to Indian philosophy, but that of "expanding form" also recurs frequently in mythology, and has been recognized in certain masterpieces of visual art. It is perhaps appropriate to quote the words of Heinrich Zimmer (my italics): "The notion that there is nothing static, nothing abiding, but only the flow of a relentless process, *with everything originating, growing, decaying, vanishing* – this wholly dynamic view of life, of the individual and of the universe, is one of the fundamental conceptions of later Hinduism."[7] This conception has frequently been translated into artistic terms, for example in the 6th century relief of the expanding Viṣṇu, from Bādāmī, about which the same author writes: 'The quality of time permeates the inert matter of the stone. Flow and growth transform the mineral substance into an organism interminably expanding.'[8] Perhaps the similar effect of the musical *trikāla* technique is suggested by the word *trikāla* itself, which can also refer to the "three times" – past, present and future.

---

[6] Close study of the ornamentation reveals a certain reluctance, especially on the part of the violinist, to dwell on either A♭ , or F, even in the quicker versions of the melody (see e.g. bar 5, violin, 5th quaver; bar 27, flute and violin, 13th crotchet; etc.).

[7] Heinrich Zimmer, *Myths and Symbols in Indian Art and Civilization* (Princeton, 1972), p.131.

[8] *op. cit.* p.132.

In conclusion it may be said that in the Trikāla the musicians demonstrate not only their astonishing rhythmic virtuosity, but also the dramatic and structural possibilities of the augmentation-diminution technique: possibilities which perhaps merit greater attention on the part of Western composers.

Notes on the transcription

In order to show the melodic and rhythmic structure as clearly as possible, the outline of the melody played by the flute and violin has been presented on a single staff, in a simplified form without ornamentation. Above this the complete flute and violin parts are shown in a notation which can only be approximate. The mṛdaṅgam part is represented below the melodic outline; the many sounds of the instrument are grouped approximately according to pitch — high, medium or low.

Below the mṛdaṅgam part the hand-claps, the underlying tāla pattern, and a semiquaver time-scale are represented on a single line. Marks at regular intervals, representing semiquavers at MM 360 approximately, are replaced by notes on the third and fifth quavers of each tāla-cycle, representing the hand-claps, and by rests on the other main beats. The melodic outline and the mṛdaṅgam part are divided throughout into bars corresponding to the original division of the melody into tāla-cycles at the outset of the piece; short bar-lines between the staves represent the internal division of each cycle. Each change of tempo in the melody is marked by a double bar and a new time-signature (note-values remain the same throughout, as is shown by the semiquaver time-scale).

TRIKĀLA

Rāga : Śaṅkarābharaṇam
Tāla : Miśra Cāpu

*Sounds 1 octave higher

68

69

70

72

73

Duration 2'43"

The genesis of carvel-built lutes

HARVEY TURNBULL

(Trinity College, Cambridge)

The shape, method of construction and size of the resonator, and the materials used in its fabrication, are among the more important features of lutes, as these largely determine sound quality. The acceptance or rejection of any particular morphological or ergological feature will often depend on what is locally regarded as the ideal sound for the instrument, but any aetiological account of the evolution of lutes must also consider the local availability of materials and prevailing technology. The evidence of folk lutes with gourd or carapace resonators, which are found in areas where cucurbits and tortoises are readily available, suggests the constant use of natural vessels for the bodies of lutes.[1] When wood is used for the resonator, two types of construction can be distinguished. In the one the body is carved from a block of wood (carved body), while in the other it is assembled from separate pieces of wood. These can be arranged to form a flat-backed instrument (for example, the guitar) or a round-backed instrument (for example, the *'ūd* or the European lute). In the latter case a number of uniformly thin strips of wood (ribs) are carefully shaped and bent to form the domed back (carvel-built body). This method achieves (in general) a much lighter structure than the carved body; the weight of a carvel-built body is similar to that of the gourd resonator of, for example, a Hindustani sitar.

Curt Sachs regarded the carved body as the first stage in the development of lutes.[2] He argued further that the process of carving gave rise to two new features. The first was that the originally spherical body became egg-shaped; this came about since it was possible to carve body and neck as an integrated whole, with the body tapering towards the neck. The second consequence was that 'the body lost its strongly rounded shape and showed the smooth chamfers (*Abfasungen*)[3] of the knife.' Furthermore, Sachs was of the opinion that

---

[1] The British Museum possesses a tortoise shell with the remains of leather bindings (Museum No. 38171), which was originally the body of a long-necked lute. Found in Egypt, the carapace dates from the New Kingdom, *c.*1300 B.C.

[2] *Real-Lexicon der Musikinstrumente,* revised edition, New York, 1964, entry *Tanbūr.*

[3] I am grateful to Rembrandt Wolpert of Peterhouse, Cambridge for helping me with the meaning of *Abfasungen* (which does not appear in the German dictionaries I consulted) and the implications of the term in the context of a carved lute body.

'according to the Law of Preservation valid also, and at all times, for the history of instruments, these chamfers have been preserved to the present day in lutes in the form of ribs (*Späne*).' He defines *Späne* as: the ribs of stringed instruments without side-walls (*Zargen*), with an angular contour (*kantig gearbeitet*).[4] The figures below show the different contours in cross-section of (a) a gourd sliced longitudinally and (b) the chamfered, carved body, envisaged by Sachs as anticipating a carvel-built body:

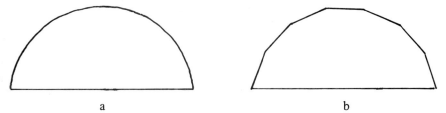

a   b

There is much to object to in these assumptions. First, natural objects that can be used as resonators are not necessarily spherical. Gourds grow naturally in a variety of shapes, one of which is spheroidal, but both waisted and flask-shaped types occur. Again, a tortoise carapace will yield a multi-faceted body with an irregularly polygonal table (Plate1,a and b). Secondly, the way in which a carved lute body is fashioned is very different from the method Sachs had in mind. This presupposes that the carver, using a knife, cuts consistently longitudinally, and with long curved strokes, to achieve the even chamfers of fig. 1 b. In fact, the shaping of the back is done with an adze, or a range of adzes, and, because of the resistance of the wood, the cutting strokes are short. Further, these are executed at all angles, and the resulting cuts do not yield the regular longitudinal chamfers envisaged by Sachs. An illustration of *Usta* (master-craftsman) Usman Zufarov, working on an Uzbek rubab[5], shows the outer surface of a lute-body; from its multi-faceted surface it is clear that the cuts followed no one direction. Finally, Sachs does not distinguish between the methods used in the production of the two types of body. As well as adzes, the maker of a carved body may also use a variety of gouges. On the other hand, in preparing the wood for the ribs, the carvel-builder achieves the desired uniform thinness by planing. The advantage of the plane is 'that it takes off a continuous shaving, instead of the chips removed by tools like the axe or adze, chisel of knife.'[6] A second, necessary, technical accomplishment is the ability to bend the thin strips of wood to the curvature required in order to assemble a hemispherical body; this is done with heat, either by steaming or by using a hot iron. The likelihood, then, of a carver generating (as Sachs postulated) a body that would suggest carvel building is remote; if there were, or are, any such

[4]   *op.cit.* entry *Spähne* (*sic*).

[5]   Alexander Buchner, *Folk Music Instruments of the World,* Prague, 1971, Plate 207; the maker is not identified, but he is also featured in R.L. Sadokov, *Muzikal'naya Kultura Drevnego Khorezma,* Moscow, 1970, p.42.

[6]   W.L. Goodman, *The History of Woodworking Tools,* London, 1964, p.40.

Plate 1a

Plate 1b

carved instruments with chamfered surfaces, they must have been modelled on a carvel-built lute and not *vice versa.*

It seems certain, therefore, that carvel-building was not prompted by a carved proto-type. The question as to the origin of this more delicate method of construction remains unanswered. Although the gourd has often been cited as a *morphological* determinant of the shapes of lutes, its role as an *ergological* determinant in their construction has not hitherto been considered. The internal anatomy of the gourd,[7] and the fact that it was constantly in the hands of instrument makers, in areas where cucurbits were available, suggest, however, that it may itself have provided the model for carvel construction. Inside the gourd are three seed-masses surrounded by pulp. Once these are removed, a ribbed patterning of the inner wall is disclosed (Plate 2); this is visible even when the outer surface is quite smooth. Thus, when the maker wished to produce, in wood, a body that would compare favourably with the lighter gourd, he already had before him a natural model suggesting a means by which to achieve this end, namely by glueing together spheroidal segments.

The earliest unambiguously explicit reference to a carvel-built lute occurs in the *Ikhwān al-Safa'*,[8] a tenth century collection of Arabic writings on science and philosophy. The author of the treatise on music (in that collection) comments on the *'ūd* that 'its boards (*alwāḥ*) should be thin and made from light wood.' How far back this tradition extended is not known, but indirect evidence suggests that carvel-built bodies may have been known to the Arabs in the ninth century and perhaps as early as the end of the eighth. Al-Kindī (d.c. 874), while not referring specifically to segmental construction of the body, lays great stress on uniform thinness of the wood, when writing about the *'ūd*: 'It is necessary that its soundchest be as thin as possible, and that this should be general, so that there is not in the back any place thinner nor thicker than any other place. And likewise in its belly, because a difference in the thinness or thickness of its parts would interfere with the evenness of the [sound of the] strings and the concord of the notes.'[9] On the occasion of his first audition before Hārūn al-Rashīd (786-809), Ziryab is reported as having refused to play the lute of his teacher, Isḥāq al-Mausilī, preferring his own, which he said was of a different structure.[10] It is significant that, although Ziryab's lute was of the same size as the lute generally played, it was one third lighter.[11] Uniform thinness and lightness,

---

[7]   See addendum 'A note on the morphology of gourds.'

[8]   Henry George Farmer. 'The Structure of the Arabian and Persian Lute in the Middle Ages,' *Journal of the Royal Asiatic Society,* 1939, p.45; in a footnote Farmer states of *alwāḥ* that 'this refers to the slender strips of wood, graduated at the extremities, out of which the beautiful arched back of the lute was made.'

[9]   tr. by Farmer, *op.cit.* p.44; the 'concord' of the notes would not be affected by the thinness of the wood if the term refers to agreement in pitch.

[10]   Farmer, *A History of Arabian Music to the XIIIth Century,* London, 1929, reprinted 1967, p.219.

[11]   Farmer, 'The Structure', p.42.

Plate 2

together with mention of a different structure, suggest a carvel-built body. On present evidence the Arabs must be regarded as the inventors of carvel-built lutes.

The carving/hollowing out traditional method of producing a lute body is much older than the carvel-building technique. However, the necessary technology for the latter process was known many centuries before the period when Arabic writers first commented on it. The plane is first mentioned in Ancient Greece,[12] although the earliest extant specimens are Roman, dating from the first century A.D.[13] Bending wood by heat has a yet longer history.[14] A reference in the *Rig Veda* reveals that this was practised by the Aryan invaders of India to produce felloes for wheels; V. Gordon Childe suggests that the technique 'was diffused between the Ganges and the Rhine, together with Indo-European languages, by our half-mythical linguistic ancestors, the Indo-Europeans.' By 500 B.C., Celtic wainwrights in Bohemia and the Rhineland were using a single length of wood for the felloe, bending it by heat; an earlier example of this technique appears in the wheels of an Egyptian chariot from Thebes (1500 B.C.).[14] Theophrastus records that 'in general those woods which are tough are easy to bend';[15] it has been suggested that this was probably achieved by steaming.[16]

The process of bending wood by heat is not without its drawbacks:[17] 'Creating curved forms by steaming and bending wood is an ancient, laborious and not entirely satisfactory process. Only certain woods, such as ash and beech, take kindly to the process. Even with suitable woods, considerable waste occurs in selecting for straightness of grain and freedom from knots; a further high percentage of waste inevitably occurs through fibre rupture in bending, the percentage rising in ratio to the thickness of the timber to be bent. Moreover, unless the design of the object allows for the bend to be held after it is formed, the curvature must be made sharper than required, so as to allow for the thrust which the compressed side of the bend exerts'. The comparatively late appearance of carvel-built lutes may be due to these difficulties. However, this is unlikely, as, in spite of the lack of indigenous supplies of timber in Southern and Eastern Mediterranean countries, the craftsman there continually refined his wood-working techniques. Indeed, scarcity of wood resulted in the achievement of skills more advanced than those of a thickly forested region (such as Northern

[12] Theophrastus, *De historia plantarium,* tr. Sir Arthur Hort, *The History of Plants,* London, 1916, Vol. II, p.455.

[13] W.L. Goodman, *loc. cit.*

[14] V. Gordon Childe, 'Rotary Motion', *A History of Technology,* Vol. I, ed. Charles Singer, E.J. Holmyard and A.R. Hall, Oxford, 1954, p.212; see also pp.727-8.

[15] *op.cit.* p.453.

[16] Cyril Aldred, 'Furniture to the End of the Roman Empire', *A History of Technology,* Vol. II, ed. C. Singer, E.J. Holmyard, A.R. Hall and T.I. Williams, Oxford, 1956, p.234.

[17] Edward H. Pinto, *The Craftsman in Wood,* London, 1962, p.161.

Europe) which (in Medieval times) were still based on the axe, adze, and knife, as opposed to the saw, chisel, and plane, of the Mediterranean world; 'a carpenter's technique as distinct from a joiner's.'[18]

A more likely explanation of the tardy appearance of carvel-built lutes is that, until the rise of the '$\bar{u}d$ to a dominant position in Islamic music, there was no incentive to experiment with methods of improving the sonority of lutes. In Medieval times the '$\bar{u}d$ was the most popular instrument of the Arabs, and their theory of music was expounded in terms of its frets. Consequently, it is not surprising that they would wish to make it as responsive an instrument as possible.

The carvel-built construction of the '$\bar{u}d$ confers on it a unique position among the lutes of the Middle Ages. The extant instruments, and literary references, reveal that the practice of medieval lute builders was to make the instruments in two parts; the body, neck, and peg-board, were carved from a single block of wood, and the belly was fixed over the body cavity.[19] There was no appreciation of the texture and appearance of wood, the grain of which was often hidden under coats of brightly-coloured paint.[20]

The lack of evidence of carvel-building in medieval lutes, apart from the '$\bar{u}d$, suggests that when this method of construction was adopted for the European lute — ultimately to become the most highly esteemed plucked instrument of the Renaissance — it was as a consequence of direct borrowing from the Arabs, and not as a result of any indigenous development. The state of medieval European wood-working technology supports this view. In spite of finds of small planes from the Dark Ages,[21] the general standard of woodworking has led to the view that the plane did not reappear in Europe until

---

[18]   Cyril Adred, *op.cit.* p.236.

[19]   Werner Bachmann, *The Origins of Bowing*, London, 1962, p.72; Frederick Crane, *Extant Medieval Musical Instruments: A Provisional Catalogue by Types*, Iowa City, 1972, p.15, comments 'The one-piece construction is shared by virtually all medieval string instruments except harps; in this respect they find their closest modern relatives in the European folk instruments, as the art-music instruments have long had bodies constructed of several pieces.'

[20]   Friedrich Dick, 'Bezeichungen für Saiten- und Schlaginstrumente in der altfranzösischen Literatur', *Giessener Beiträge zur romanischen Philologie*, No.25, 1932, p.63, quotes *2 guiternes de boys, l'une painte de rouge à feuillages de jaulne* and *l'autre est de boys blanc*; R.W. Symonds, 'Furniture: Post Roman', *A History of Technology*, Vol.II, p.247, mentions that 'Medieval peoples, particularly those under dull northern skies, loved bright colours, and it seems never to have occurred to them to admire the natural grain of woods.'

[21]   W.L. Goodman, *op.cit.* pp.54-6; A number of small planes from Frisia in Holland and one from Kent provide 'a thin but continuous link between the Roman period and the Middle Ages.' Goodman comments on a reconstruction of the small Kent plane, 'The tool is remarkably easy to use, and resembles the small violin planes described in Edward Heron-Allen's *Violin-making.*' The planes from the Dark Ages range from 5½" to 8½" in length; the iron of the Kent plane is only ¾" wide. These are much smaller and cruder than the Roman planes. They are, however, larger than those

the twelfth century.[22] There is an isolated reference to bending wood by heat, but not in a way that would suggest its use in lute building.[23]

Europe benefitted in many ways from the body of knowledge inherited by the Arabs: 'In much the same way that Muslim scholars transmitted to posterity a large fund of ancient learning, Muslim artisans preserved, developed and spread abroad the traditional "workshop practice" of arts current in the Orient, which had neither penetrated into Europe or, if known there in former times, had decayed during the period of storm and stress that ushered in the Middle Ages.'[24] The technique of carvel-building in lutes should be included among the skills that were introduced in medieval times, with important consequences for the European instrumentarium. It is significant that carvel-building was extended to the guitar[25] and became a permanent feature of the *chitarra battente,* instruments that, with their waisting, do not lend themselves readily to construction with a rounded back. Carvel-building skills would also have found application in the construction of the guitar and other instruments, such as those of the viol/violin family, where similar curvature is demanded.

described by Heron-Allen; these are oval planes in three sizes, the largest of which is no more than an inch or so in length (*Violin-making, as it was and is,* London, 1884, p.222, figs.124 and 125, which show the actual sizes of the planes), and an oblong plane 2" x ½" (*op.cit.* p.225, fig.136, actual size). The oval planes are only used to smooth the marks left by the gouge in the belly and back (*op.cit.* p.242). The small size of the planes from the Dark Ages would limit their application and they would not be suitable for thinning the large sheets of wood that lute construction would demand.

[22] e.g. *The History of Technology,* Vol.II, p.641.

[23] The reference, to a stick that can be easily bent when moistened and placed in warm ashes, is quoted by F.M. Feldhaus, *Die Technik der Vorzeit, der geschichtlichen Zeit und der Naturvölker,* Leipzig and Berlin, 1914, p.531, on the authority of a fragment by Theophilus found in the *Lumen Animae,* Augsburg, 1477. Feldhaus' source is the translation by Albert Ilg, *Theophilus Presbyter Schedula Diversarum Artium,* Vol.VII of *Quellenschriften für Kunstgeschichte,* Vienna, 1874, where the relevant passages can be found on pp.360-1 and pp.366-7. The 1477 *Lumen Animae* was edited by Matthias Farinator from a manuscript, now lost, of the late thirteenth or early fourteenth century (Lynn Thorndike, *A History of Magic and Experimental Science,* Vol.III, New York, 1934, p.552). Modern commentators (Thorndike, *op.cit.* p.553 and C.R. Dodwell, in the introduction to his translation of Theophilus' *De Diversis Artibus,* London, 1961, p.xlv) have pointed out that the supposed Theophilus quotations do not come from *De Diversis Artibus* and are quite unlike it in tone. Dodwell has suggested (*op.cit.* pp.1-1i) that the original compiler of the *Lumen Animae* may have worked from a copy of *De Diversis Artibus* that was bound with other works and in which there was no differentiation between the text of Theophilus and that of other authors. As yet the pseudo-Theophilus statements have not been attributed to a definite source.

[24] A.H. Christie, 'Islamic Minor Arts and their Influence upon European Work', *The Legacy of Islam,* ed. Sir Thomas Arnold and Alfred Guillaume, Oxford, 1931, p.111.

[25] Harvey Turnbull, *The Guitar from the Renaissance to the Present Day,* London, 1974, pp.11-12, where the influences of the Renaissance lute on the four-course guitar are considered.

ADDENDUM: A NOTE ON THE MORPHOLOGY OF GOURDS

by L. E. R. PICKEN

If a full description of the anatomy, both gross and microscopic, and of the developmental history, of the fruit of the Bottle Gourd, *Lagenaria siceraria* (Molina) Standl, exists, it has as yet proved impossible to find, either by reference to recent authorities (Whitaker and Davis, 1962; Purseglove, 1968) or to the standard work of Saunders (1939) on floral morphology. There can be no doubt, however, that the pattern of longitudinal striations, observed by Mr. Turnbull and displayed in his Plate 2 (showing the interior surface of the wall of an Ornamental Gourd (*Cucurbita pepo* L. var. *ovifera* (L.) Alef), is a pattern of peripheral vascular bundles, lying immediately internal to the fibrous (sclerenchymatous) layer that forms the rigid wall of the mature gourd. For *Cucumis sativus* L. (the cucumber), Purseglove (Figure 17E, opposite p.116, *Dicotelydons 1,* op.cit.) shows nine such bundles, three to each of the carpels of the gynaeceum. Though the latter is commonly trimerous, pentamerous symmetry occurs in some members of the Cucurbitaceae, and in the loofah (*Luffa cylindrica* (L.) M.J. Roem), for example, change from the pentamerous to the trimerous condition may occur between the proximal and distal ends of one and the same specimen. The number of peripheral vascular bundles is in fact usually ten, as shown by observations on transected cucumbers, and on courgettes (*Cucurbita pepo* var. *medullosa* Alef). In these fruits, the vascular bundles underlie the ten external ridges.

In *Lagenaria* fruits (the gourd most commonly used in the making of lutes), where external ridges are absent, the number of internal striae is about 20. The figures suggest that a primary system of ten vascular bundles is doubled in the fruit of the Bottle Gourd.

A minor point, but one of structural interest, is the fact that, in cucumbers and courgettes, the bulk of each of these conspicuous vascular bundles is largely taken up by a single, enormous vessel, the diameter of which approaches 1 mm. In the loofah, however, no trace of this superficial and primary system of longitudinal vascular bundles is to be seen, since it is removed, along with the epidermis and immediately subepidermal tissues, in the process of preparing the loofah from the ripe fruit.

It is to be stressed that the primary pattern of vascular bundles visible on the inner face of the wall of the Bottle Gourd is superficial in relation to the substance of the wall. Though it may well have inspired (as Mr. Turnbull plausibly suggests) the carvel-building of lute-bodies, it marks no mechanical segmentation of the rigid wall in the natural object; it is a mere vestige of the archaic circulatory system of the carpels.

Purseglove, J. *Tropical Crops, Dicotyledons 1,* 1968, London.

Whitaker, T.W., and Davis, G.N., *Cucurbits* (World Crops Series), 1962, London.

Saunders, E.R., *Floral Morphology,* a new outlook with special reference to the interpretation of the gynaeceum, volume I, 1937; volume II, 1939, Cambridge.

The shapes of the *Shi Jing*[1] song-texts and their musical implications

LAURENCE PICKEN

(Jesus College, Cambridge)

Glancing through the song-texts of the Shi Jing as they appear on the printed page in any edition of that collection, the only obvious difference between them is that some are longer than others. The stimulus to inquire further into possible differences came initially from the work of Dobson[2] on line-sharing between songs[3]. In the course of examining the song-texts, it was realized that two-dimensional diagrams of the songs would make it more readily possible to compare song-forms and relative durations. Accordingly graphs were made in which line- and stanza-structure are displayed along the abscissa, and stanza-sequence along the ordinate. The resulting diagrams (text-figures 1-5) are to be read as 'silent music' — as compound rhythmic patterns of three superimposed rhythms: lexigraph-rhythm, line-rhythm, and stanza-rhythm. A stanza is shown as a transverse strip of standard depth, vertically subdivided by thicker lines that mark the ends of lines, and by thinner lines that separate the monosyllabic words of the text. In each case, one begins reading at the bottom left-hand corner and follows the syllable-pulses from line to line to the right, throughout a stanza, along the abscissa. Lines are numbered horizontally in Arabic numerals within a stanza; stanzas are numbered from the first stanza onwards vertically up the ordinate in Roman numerals. *Both* axes are time-axes, but the abscissa represents stanza-duration (measured in a sequence of text-lines), while the ordinate represents song-duration (measured as a sequence of text-stanzas). Initial and final syllables of stanzas are cross-hatched to indicate that they are necessarily musically different in some way from other syllables, so that initial (i) and final (f) lines are musically different from medial (m) lines. In general, initial lines will have a 'setting-out' musical character; final lines, a 'returning home' character.

---

1   詩 經

---

2   W.A.C.H. Dobson, *The Language of the Book of Songs.* (Toronto, 1968).

3   L.E.R. Picken, 'The Musical Implications of Line-Sharing in the Book of Songs (*Shih Ching*)', *Journal of the American Oriental Society*, 89 (1969), pp.408-10.

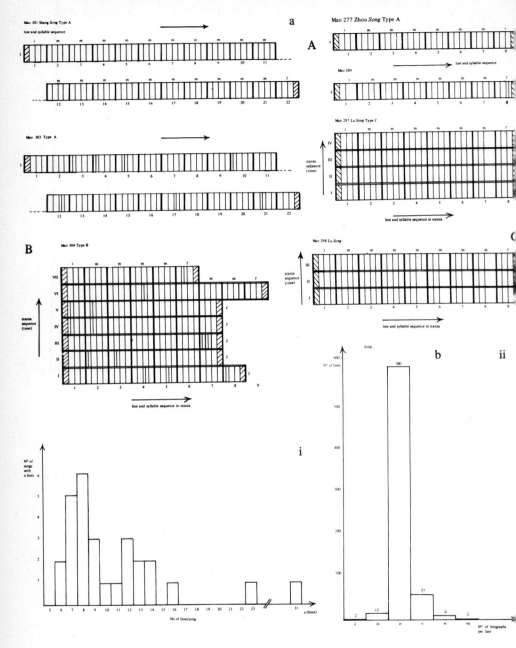

Fig. 1   Shang, Lu, and Zhou *song*:

    a   Duration diagrams — Types A, B, and C

    b   i   Frequency polygon — numbers of songs with x lines per song

          ii   Frequency polygon — number of lines with x lexigraphs per line. 87 per cent of all the lines are lines of four lexigraphs.

86

ASSUMPTIONS AND HYPOTHESES

Dobson has argued that the praise-songs — the *song*[4] — ascribed to the States of Shang, Zhou and Lu, are later compositions than those of the sections Da Ya[5], Xiao Ya[6] and Guo Feng[7]. This view is shared by Barnard,[8] who has proposed a radically later date for the entire Shi Jing text. Even though the *song* be archaising fabrications, however, they are not without interest as evidence of hypotheses about ancient song, current in later Zhou times. It is striking that the shapes of Shang, Zhou and Lu *song*, plotted as previously indicated, differ markedly from each other, as shown in Figure 1a. In these and other diagrams, it has been assumed (1) that the predominantly 4-syllable line was also a musical measure of four equal time-units — of four 'beats', and that these songs were measured; (2) that they were sung in strict time with a steady pulse carried by notes of equal duration, save for occasional halving or doubling of the unit of duration; (3) that first and last notes of a song are likely to have been the same note (the final) or its octave; (4) that first and last notes of a stanza will also have been the same note or its octave. These assumptions (to be defended later) are based on the structure of the twelve tunes for song-texts from Xiao Ya and Guo Feng preserved by Zhu Xi[9] which, though not earlier (in all probability) than the Tang period, represent an important tradition concerning the melody-type of ritual tunes, a tradition in part reflected today in the tunes of the Confucian ritual as still practised in Taiwan and Korea. Furthermore, these assumptions are in accordance with reconstructions (as they appear to be) of ritual melodies printed by Prince Zhu Zaiyu[10]. The melody

4   頌

5   大 雅

6   小 雅

7   國 風

8   Noel Barnard, 'Metre and rhyme in the Ch'u silk manuscript text and other pre-Han archaeological documents', *28th International Congress of Orientalists.* (Canberra, 1971).

9   See L.E.R. Picken, 'Twelve Ritual Melodies of the T'ang Dynasty' , *Studia Memoriae Belae Bartók Sacra* (Budapest, 1956, 1957), pp.147-73.

10   朱 載 堉 ： 律 呂 精 義 內 篇   , j.6,7; 律 呂 精 義 外 篇 , j. 2, 3, 5-9; 操 縵 古 樂 譜   ; 旋 宮 合 樂 譜 ， 鄉 飲 詩 樂 譜   (none published before 1606 — see F.A. Kuttner: 'Prince Chu Tsai-yu's life and work' *Ethnomusicology,* XIX, pp.163-206, Ann Arbor, Michigan, 1975).

type lives on today in the sung mantras of Taoists of the *Hongtou*[11] variety, and in the melodies of ballads from Chao-zhou[12]. Lastly, such tunes are of an ancient melody-type represented in folksong and ritual melody not only in East, South, and South-East Asia,[13] but also throughout Eurasia and indeed in North Africa. The resemblance between *canti fermi* of gamelan pieces from Java and Bali, and Chinese ritual melodies, is particularly striking, especially in their through-composed character. This last appears to be an ancient feature of Chinese ritual tunes, judging by the survivals in Zhu Xi.

CHANT AND SONG

To avoid confusion, it may be well to state explicitly that there is no difference, necessarily, between the statement: "The Shi were sung as measured songs," and the statement: "The Shi were chanted." Syllabic *chant,* in which a syllable is sung to a note, is more often than not 'measured', in the sense of being sung to a steady pulse of equal beats. The judgement as to when measured, syllabic 'chant' becomes 'song' is largely subjective. 'Chant' usually carries implications of monotony (in the literal sense), that is, of sustained recitation on a given reciting note to which the voice rises in the incipit and from which the voice descends at the cadence. However, both in Buddhist[14] and Taoist practice today there are many examples of measured, syllabic chant that are not monotone; they may be chants on three notes, for example. But their texts are invariably prose texts of varying line lengths; and though one feels a pulse one does not feel a measure. Were the text to be segmented into lines of equal numbers of syllables, however, such a chant would automatically become measured and would satisfy the criteria of measured 'song'. However small the set of notes to which the Shi were sung, I prefer to regard them as having been sung rather than chanted.

While it was formerly customary to regard Ancient Chinese verse as composed largely of lines of four monosyllabic words, there is evidence, both from meaning and from structure, that the unit was frequently one of eight syllables. In the Chu silk manuscript and in certain inscriptions of the 4th

---

11　紅頭　; John Levy, *Chinese Taoist Music,* Lyrichord Stereo LLST 7223, Bd II, 2

(171). *Zhou* 冘 of the same character were recorded by L.E.R.P. from Qiu Yishu

丘一書 *Daoshi* 道士 in the Cheng Huang Miao 城隍廟 in Xinzhu

新竹 , Taiwan, on June 2, 1972.

12　潮州　; Piet van der Loon, private recording, 1965.

13　L.E.R. Picken, Chapter III, in *The New Oxford History of Music,* Volume 1, Oxford (1957). See p.168 *et seq.*

14　John Levy, *Chinese Buddhist Music,* Lyrichord Stereo LLST 7222, Bds 1, 2, 3 (1971).

century B.C. Barnard[15] finds that '8-character measures' are those mainly employed; moreover, in the sharing of lines between song-texts of the Shi Jing it is not uncommon for two 4-lexigraph units to be shared, as if the functional unit were indeed one of eight syllables. (A line-unit of this size − eight syllables − is common to Sanskrit verse, to the Avestan Hymns to Mithra, to ancient Christian hymns − such as the *Dies irae,* to certain Hungarian folk songs − where it seems to reflect eastern elements[16], and to the folk song of Bedouin tribes[17].)

EVIDENCE THAT THE SHI WERE SUNG

It may be asked: why should not these song-texts have been sung as *unmeasured* syllabic or melismatic chant, or as a mixture of both styles? The fact that learning to participate in singing Guo Feng and Xiao Ya songs at provincial banquets was a normal part of education for the gentry[18], however, argues for their being *measured* songs, as does the association of part[19] of this repertory with ritual movement, if not with dance. Measured song is easier for a group to sing in unison than unmeasured song. It is probable, moreover, that melismatic song was a late development in China, indeed a post-Song development[20]. The hypothesis that the Shi were sung as *unmeasured*, syllabic chant, of small melodic range, and sung in equal or unequal notes, is tenable; but only if one supposes (improbably) that the verse-structure has no musical significance whatsoever. The phenomenon of line-sharing,[2] with its striking resemblance to the procedure of 'centonization'[21] (= patchwork) in the construction of plainchant and Byzantine chant, suggests that the Shi Jing songs too developed as structures consisting of verbal text indissolubly wedded to

---

[15]   Noel Barnard, 'Rhyme and Metre in the Ch'u Silk Manuscript Text', *Papers on Far Eastern History,* (1971), pp.73-113.

[16]   Bence Szabolcsi, 'The Eastern relations of early Hungarian folk-music...', *Journal of the Royal Asiatic Society* (1936), pp.483-98.

[17]   J.R. Smart, 'A Bedouin Song from the Egyptian Western Desert', *Journal of Semitic Studies,* 12. (1967) pp.245-67.

[18]   朱熹 : 大戴儀禮經傳通解   , j. 14 詩樂 , 24, 1223 (呂氏寶誥堂 , c.1700). The commentary states that certain songs are sung 'nowadays' (*jin* 今) on such occasions.

[19]   A.W. Waley, *The Book of Songs.* (London, 1937). See pp.218-225.

[20]   L.E.R. Picken, 'A twelfth-century secular Chinese song in zither tablature', *Asia Major,* 16 (1971), pp.102-20.

[21]   The term itself originated with P. Ferreti, *Estetica Gregoriana* (Rome, 1934). Egon Wellesz described a similar principle of composition operative in the construction of Byzantine chant. See Egon Wellesz, *Eastern Elements in Western Chant* (Oxford, 1947), Chap. II.

musical lines. That songs were indeed sung is explicit in certain of the song-texts themselves — see for example, Mao Nos. 56, 85, 113, 149, 155, 204, 208, 220, 252. That the Shi themselves were sung is attested by the text of Mao No. 208, with its reference to the performance of Ya and Nan[22]; and the Zuo Zhuan[23] (to be regarded as a pre-Han work)[24] relates impressions produced by various sections of the Shi Jing in performance[25]. This remarkable passage occurs in the commentary to the brief statement in the Chunqiu[26] concerning the visit of the Gongzi Ja[27] of Wu[28] to Xiang[29], Duke of Lu. On that occasion: '[The Gongzi Ja of Wu] asked to hear the music of Zhou; and [the Duke of Lu] caused musicians to sing for him Zhou-Nan and Shao-Nan...' For him they sang, in due course, the entire Shi Jing in sequence, from the Guo Feng to the Song — surely to be regarded (as is the Mao order) as a sequence of increasing potency. It would appear doubtful that such a performance ever occurred, since even at a moderate pace of $\rule{0pt}{0pt}\quad$ = 90 — that is, 90 words to the minute, the complete repertory would probably demand between ten and fifteen hours to recite. Nevertheless, this report establishes that, according to a tradition that survived into pre-Han times, the repertory was indeed a repertory of songs. From the Ja's comments on the various sections of the Shi Jing, it is difficult to extract any clear-cut observations relating to musical qualities rather than to ethos; but there are two remarks that might, perhaps, be of significance. One is the statement regarding the songs of Zheng:[30] 'How beautiful! Their subtleties are

22　南

23　左傳

24　Bernhard Karlgren, 'The Early History of the Chou Li and Tso Chuan Texts', *Bulletin of the Museum of Far Eastern Antiquities,* No. 3 (Stockholm, 1931).

25　James Legge, *The Chinese Classics,* Vol. V. Part II, The Ch'un Ts'ew with the Tso Chuen, Book IX, Year XXIX, pp.545-50 (Hong Kong, 1872).

　　吳 子 使 札 來 聘。(請 觀 於 周 樂。使 工 為 之 歌
　　周 南 召 南。)

26　春 秋

27　公 子 札

28　吳

29　襄

30　鄭

90

excessive'[31], where xi might fairly be regarded as having structural implications ('their minutiae' as Legge has it). (In view of the scandalous reputation of the songs of Zheng, it is surely remarkable that the Gongzi Ja should exclaim: 'How beautiful!') The other is the statement made about the Da Ya: qu er you zhi ti[32] 'winding and yet straight-bodied' — Legge translates: 'Amid all the winding the movement is straight-forward'. This might be descriptive of a melody, twisting and turning, and yet with an overall sense of direction towards an end. A somewhat similar statement in relation to the *song* is more difficult to rationalize: qu er bu ju[33], translated by Legge as 'winding but no bending'.

It is not necessary that the number of different pitches, or the compass, should have been large for the songs to have been sung. Indeed a minimum of two notes would suffice for an incipit, a reciting tone, and a cadence: abbb: bbbb: bbba; but in such a chant-structure — corresponding to the simplest type of syllabic Gregorian chant — the mnemonic value of the music as vehicle is minimal — only first and last lines of stanzas are made more memorable by melodic associations, and there is no element to remind the singers of the number or sequence of lines and stanzas, for example.

Neolithic and Shang burials containing a set of three lithophonic stones[34] provide evidence of a minimum of three notes as a potential basis for instrumental accompaniment of ritual music of the earliest period. If there are three notes, the maximum number of different sequences of three notes taken four at a time is $3^4 = 81$. This total allows for *all* sequences, including one note being repeated four times. Any restrictions placed on the nature of the sequence — for example, the condition of non-consecutive repetition of a note — greatly reduce the number of possibilities. Supposing that the musical language of the time permitted a line of four monosyllabic words to be sung to a set of notes such that each note was used at least once, and the set included the same note twice, but not in sequence — for example: *d f g f* — three stones could have furnished eighteen different arrangements of four notes for use in medial melodic lines. This total is reached as follows: In medial position, the musical line can begin on any one of three notes. This reduces the choice of the note for second place to two notes; for third place, to one note; and the fourth place again has a choice of two — that is, any one of the three, other than the preceding note: $3 \times 2 \times 1 \times 2 = 12$. This particular sequence only allows for

31   美哉其細己甚

32   曲而有直體

33   曲而不倨

34   李純一，中國古代音樂史考，音樂出版
社   , Peking, 1957.

repetition in *either* first and fourth place *or* second and fourth place. If a third variant, repetition in first and third place, is added, the number of different possible lines is increased to eighteen. (In practice, the first note of a medial line is unlikely to be the same as the last note of the previous line; but this does not alter the number of possibilities.)

The total number of different arrangements for initial and final lines is twelve (six for each). This number is obtained in the same manner as before for medial lines, but with the added restriction that the initial, or final, note respectively of the line is fixed; for example, for a final line, the number of differing arrangements is the same as for a medial line, but with the choice of final note removed: $\frac{(3 \times 2 \times 1 \times 2)}{2} = 6$. This result includes all permitted non-consecutive note repetitions, namely, first and last, first and third, and second and last.[35]

If it is also assumed that *song* were musically distinguishable, one from another in both the opening and final musical lines, as well as in the sequence of medial musical lines, for each song-text, then the number of distinct songs possible will be limited by the number of different initial and final lines available. Should it be a condition for distinctness, that initial lines be wholly different, only six different songs could have existed in a given mode, starting on a given initial out of the set of three notes. Ignoring, for the moment, the question of the authenticity of the *song*, the Shi Jing includes five Shang *song*, four Lu *song* and 31 Zhou *song*. Evidently the Shang and Lu 'repertories' could each have been sung as a set of musically differentiated pieces, with a gamut of three notes only, since there are six possible initial lines. The Zhou *song* could not, however, have been sung as musically differentiated songs, if the musical possibilities were so limited.

If *three* modes were used, however, this would increase the number of possible initial musical lines to eighteen. Further, if differentiation did not rest solely on initial lines but on final lines also, three notes taken four at a time in three modes would yield 36 musically differentiated melodies in each mode — more than enough to give a distinctive melody for each of the 31 Zhou *song*. Furthermore, if account is taken of the sequence of medial lines as well, the number of possible melodies becomes increasingly large as the number of lines intervening between initial and final lines increases.[36]

[35] It can be shown that, subject to the restriction of non-consecutive repetition of notes, the number of initial or final lines of four places that can be constructed from $(n + 1)$ notes is $[(1 \times n \times n \times n) - n]$: while the corresponding number of medial lines is $([(n + 1) \times n \times n \times n] - n (n + 1))$, or $(n + 1)$ times the number of initial lines.

[36] It has recently been shown that a majority of song-tunes in the repertory of the Southern Votiak of the mid-Volga are based on three notes: *do,re, mi,* in 5/8 or 7/8 rhythms. See László Vikár, 'Votiak trichord melodies', *Studia Muscologica Academiae Scientiarum Hungaricae*, 11 (1969), pp.461-71.

SOME MUSICAL IMPLICATIONS OF THE EXISTENCE OF CHIME-IDIOPHONES IN ZHOU AND LATE ZHOU TIMES

Archaeological evidence suggests that multiplication of members in chimes of lithophones or bells did not become general until Zhou and possibly Late Zhou times – say from the beginning of the first millenium B.C., or even from 500 B.C. onwards. The first approximately complete chime to be excavated under scientific conditions is that from Changsha, with thirteen bells in a gamut of

7 is one comma sharp, 10 and 11 are semisharp and semiflat.[37] Kuttner[38] pointed out, however, that the decoration of these bells is archaic in style in relation to the date of the tomb; he suggested that the set may already have been an antique when buried in the fifth century B.C. Considering this gamut as a basis for sets of notes, it is evident that the potential for performing differentiated tunes is greatly increased. Assuming that the gapped series was used to provide different five-note sets, rather than for seven-note sets (since the five-note set appears to have been primary in China), it is evident that, even were only bells (2), (3), (4), (5), (6), (8) and (9) (that is, seven bells in all) to be in general use, at least 840 (= 7 x 6 x 5 x 4) alternative sets of four notes, not including repetitions, would have been available for use in medial positions regardless of mode. Subject to the same restrictions, the number of sets for use as initial and final lines would be 120 (= 1 x 6 x 5 x 4). With four modes, this last figure would be multiplied by four. With non-consecutive repetition of one note, initial and final lines[35] each amount to (1 x 6 x 6 x 6 – 6) = 212, medial lines[35] to (7 x 6 x 6 x 6 – 42) = 1470. These numbers of sets available imply that, by the sixth century B.C., the resources were far greater than would be necessary to provide a different tune for each of the 31 Zhou *song*.

THE FORMAL TYPES OF SHI-JING SONG-TEXTS

1   Type A:

As indicated at the outset (p.87), even though the *song* may be late Zhou fabrications, the traditions of Shang, Lu, and Zhou, are formally differentiated (see text-figure 1a). It will now be argued that the forms of these traditions were not derived exclusively by extrapolation from forms encountered in Da Ya and Xiao Ya (text-figures 2, 3).

[37]   A.D. Fokker, 'Acoustical analysis of a peal of thirteen Chinese bells', *Koninklijke Nederlandsche Akademie van Wetenschappen – Amsterdam, Proceedings, Series B,* 74 (1971) pp.257-62. Professor Fokker was concerned to point out that the tuning of these bells could not be explained in terms of 'Pythagorean Theory' alone.

[38]   F.A. Kuttner, 'A "Pythagorean" tone system in China antedating the early Greek achievements by several centuries', *Bericht über den 7. internationalen musikwissenschaftlichen Kongress/Köln* (Basel, 1958), pp.174-6.

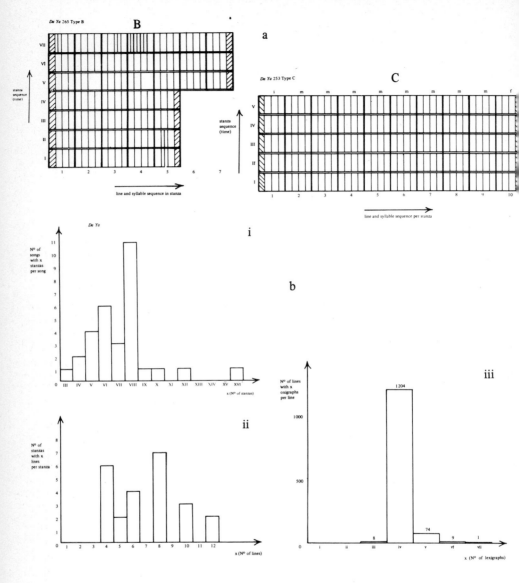

Fig. 2 Da Ya:
    a   Duration diagrams — Types B and C
    b   Frequency polygons
         i   numbers of songs with x stanzas per song. 71 per cent of the
              population have an even number of stanzas.
        ii   numbers of stanzas with x lines per stanza. 92 per cent of the
              population have an even number of lines per stanza.
       iii   numbers of lines with x lexigraphs per line. 93 per cent of the
              population have four lexigraphs per line.

The Zhou *song* (text-figure 1a) are of a type (Type A) without counterpart in the two later sections (text-figures 2-5). All Zhou *song* are non-stanzaic texts, varying in length from five to 31 lines (text-figure 1bi), and more than half the song-texts are heterometric; that is to say, they include occasional lines of more or less than four syllables. The ratio of the number of 'isometric' songs (that is, songs in which all lines are of the same length) to that of 'heterometric' songs (some lines of different length) in the Zhou *song* is 0.7. A plot of line-frequency against length of line in number of syllables, yields a skew curve with a maximum at four syllables to the line (text-figure 1bii). 87 per cent of all lines in the Zhou *song* are lines of four syllables. The most frequent deviant is the line of five syllables, amounting to some 7 per cent of the total. If a measure of four equal beats is postulated, more than four syllables could have been accommodated within that measure by halving one or more beats; less than four syllables could be accommodated by doubling the duration of one, or two, syllables. In fact, in addition to lines of four syllables, lines of two, three, five, six, and seven syllables also occur, though very infrequently.

It is remarkable that this distinctive *song*-form, consisting of a chain of predominantly 4-syllable lines — to some extent reminiscent of the undoubtedly ancient, and universal, litany-type of non-stanzaic folksong-structure — does not occur in Da Ya or Xiao Ya, or in later sections of the Shi Jing. Furthermore, one of the two types of song occurring in the Shang-*song* is an extended version of this Zhou *song* type. Though the frequency-polygon obtained on plotting (for the Zhou *song*) numbers of songs against number of lines, shows a peak at songs of eight lines, two of the Zhou *song* texts reach 23 and 31 lines respectively, a size similar to that of the Shang *song* of 22 lines (text-figure 1a, Shang *song* 303) which (like the Zhou *song*) occasionally show 5-syllable lines.

2 Type B:

A second type (Type B), represented by two specimens of Shang *song*, is also represented (unlike Type A) among songs of the Da Ya and Xiao Ya repertories. Type B is a large, heterorhythmic (p.103), stanzaic form (text-figure 1a), with about as many lines to the stanza as stanzas to the song. Again, lines of five syllables (and once of six) occur. Such a song will give a more massive, defined, and compact effect (as the shape suggests), than a song of the linear, litany-type, in listening to which attention will soon begin to wander. In listening to Type B, lines and stanzas, as well as the pulse of note-durations, will define a rhythmic structure of three different time-scales. The first stanza of Mao 304 (text-figure 1a), is one of eight lines, with rhythmic variants in lines in medial position (that is, neither initial nor final) and in the final line of the stanza. The probable musical rhythm of the variant lines can be inferred from the semantic rhythm of the text-lines (see also later, p.104). With a large-scale rhythm of 4 x 2 lines established by the first stanza, the halving of the terminal 2-line unit and anticipation of the cadence, in the next stanza, will surprise the listener; but the effect of surprise will fade with repetition during the next three stanzas. The sixth stanza, by contrast, postpones the cadence by lengthening the structure to nine lines, thus leading to an accumulation of tension in anticipation of the cadence. This tension is broken by a return to the final, short, regular stanza of 3 x 2 lines.

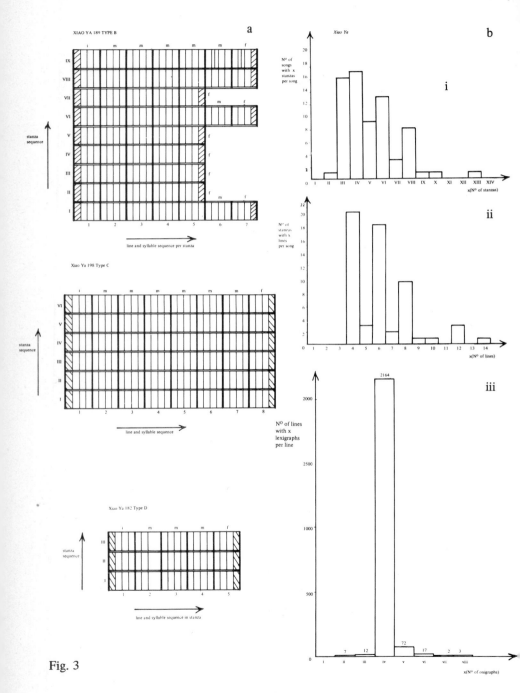

Fig. 3

3   Xiao Ya:
    a   Duration diagrams — types B, C, and D
    b   Frequency polygons
        i   numbers of songs with x stanzas per song. 59 per cent of the
             population have an even number of stanzas per song.
        ii   numbers of stanzas with x lines per stanza. 90 per cent of the
             population have an even number of lines per stanza.
        iii numbers of lines with x lexigraphs per line. 95 per cent of the
             population have four lexigraphs per line.

Mao 189 (*Xiao Ya*) (text-figure 3a) is a further example of this type, with more limited use of varying syllable-count, and Mao 265 (*Da Ya*) (text-figure 2a) may serve as an example from a nominally older part of the repertory (see Dobson). The latter example shows a wider range of variation in the number of syllables to a line — between 3 and 7. As before, lengthening a stanza in postponing a final cadence, may be expected to heighten tension and expentancy — particularly where the number of lines is odd.

3   *Types C & D:*

A third type of song from among the *song* is the one attributed to the State of Lu (text-figure 1a). It is characterized by a relatively small number of stanzas and a relatively large number of lines to the stanza (Type C). On the whole, one would expect the effect of such a structure to be more sober and less dramatic than that of Type B, previously considered. (The Lu praise-songs also include two examples of Type B, with as many stanzas as lines to the stanza namely, Mao 299 and 300: the latter song includes one stanza of 38 syllables as printed in the Harvard-Yenching Concordance.)

The Da Ya and Xiao Ya also include the Lu *song* type (Type C) (text-figures 2 and 3), and the Xiao Ya songs make extensive use of a smaller version of Type C, namely, Type D.

If we accept the view that the *song* were all inventions of later Zhou times, and that Da Ya and Xiao Ya are, notwithstanding Barnard's arguments, the first genuine texts of the Zhou, it is clearly possible that Type B of the Shang *song* could have been modelled on the same type among Da and Xiao Ya. The same is true of the songs of Types B and C among the Lu *song*; but the Zhou *song* have no formal counterpart in Da Ya and Xiao Ya.

Since songs of all three types: A, B, and C, are called *song*, it is evident that formal structure, whether of verse or of music, played no part in the definition of a *song*. Presumably, content was the essential element differentiating *song* from other songs. This renders still more remarkable, however, the fact that the praise-songs of Shang, Lu, and Zhou, are formally differentiated.

THE LITANY-TYPE *SONG* OF THE SHANG AS AN AUTHENTIC MEMORY

It may perhaps be concluded that, notwithstanding their possibly late fabrication, the *song* reflect memories of three different traditions, two of which lived on in the forms of Da Ya and Xiao Ya. Furthermore, since type A of the Zhou *song* is a type unique to the *song* (and shared with the Shang *song* tradition), it may indeed represent a real song-type, known to the early Zhou, and reflecting an ancient tradition, compatible with its archaic, litany-like form. It is highly improbable that such a form should have been a literary invention, *ex nihilo*, of the late Zhou period. If one wished to create songs (in praise of imperial ancestors, for instance) based on types such as B and C, the obvious tendency would be to compose something yet larger and more massive — *not* to revert to a simple, linear structure. It is suggested, therefore, that Type A represents a real memory of a praise-song in litany-form.

Accepting this view, however, the Shang *song* form (type A) might be interpreted as an imaginative elaboration of the (on the whole) shorter Zhou *song* type; but if type A is an historically valid type for the Zhou, the chances are that the Shang *song*, as we see them in the Shi Jing, also reflect a yet earlier tradition of praise-songs in litany-form. In short, the differences between Shang, Lu, and Zhou repertories, may reflect real differences in formal organization

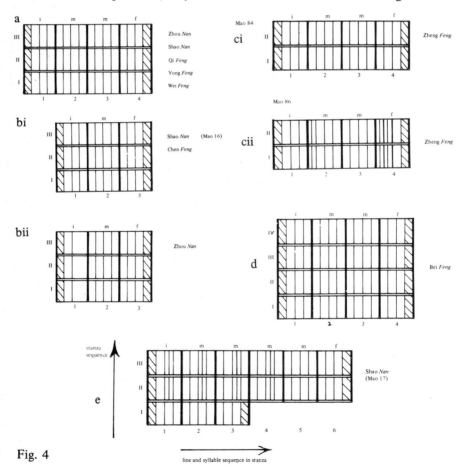

Fig. 4

line and syllable sequepce in stanza

4   Guo Feng:
     Duration diagrams — Type D
   a   Zhou Nan, Qi Feng, Shao Nan, Yong Feng, Wei Feng
   b   i   Shao Nan, Chen Feng
        ii   Zhou Nan
   c   Zheng Feng
   d   Bei Feng
   e   Shao Nan

between culturally, and to some extent ethnically, different traditions, even though the texts are from later Zhou times.

Since the preceding paragraph on the litany-type *song* of the Shang and Zhou repertories was written, Olsvai (1973)[39] (in his Introduction to Volume VI of the *Corpus Musicae Popularis Hungaricae,* and in a discussion of 'Types of Folksong') has proposed (on the basis of Hungarian materials) a generalization, strikingly appropriate to the contents of the Shi Jing, regarding the relative proportions of non-strophic and strophic tunes in the Hungarian folk-song repertory: 'The main bulk of Hungarian folk-music material consists of strophic tunes in which the number of sections is fixed. In the collection of the Hungarian Academy of Sciences, there are over one hundred thousand strophic tunes as against a few thousand tunes of loose (non-strophic) structure... The loose-structured tunes are performed on certain definite occasions..., while the strophic tunes are used to satisfy, as it were, a standing demand...'. In the Shi Jing, the *song* are not merely non-stanzaic texts, they are also praise-songs of a special kind 'for certain definite occasions'. If we interpret Olsvai's 'a few thousand' as something less than ten thousand, the ratio of strophic to non-strophic tunes in the Hungarian repertory must be of the order of 10; in the Shi Jing, the ratio of stanzaic to non-stanzaic texts is of the same order, namely, 8.

THE FORMS OF GUO-FENG SONG-TEXTS

Turning now to the formal organization of song-texts of the *Guo Feng,* (*Airs of the Principalities*) (text-figures 4 and 5), their smaller size leaps to the eye, and they are evidently to be compared with the dominant type D of the *Xiao Ya.* Assuming a constant speed of performance, a diagram of smaller area implies a song of shorter duration. Shorter stanzas mean more frequent interruption of the flow of the melody by final cadences; a sudden increase in stanza-length heightens anticipation of a cadence — the converse being felt as a surprise; and variation in the number of syllables to the line means varied rhythms for individual musical lines, and therefore a more lively tune. Two types of diagram have been prepared from data furnished by Guo Feng songs: (1) those of the same kind as are shown in text-figures 1a, 2a and 3a (text-figure 4); and (2) frequency-polygons showing the distribution of songs with from II to VI stanzas, and of stanzas with from 3 to 12 lines (text figure 5).

[39]   Pál Járdányi and Imre Olsvai, *Corpus Musicae Popularis Hungaricae,* VI, *Népdaltípusok, 1,* Budapest, 1973, p.31.

Fig. 5

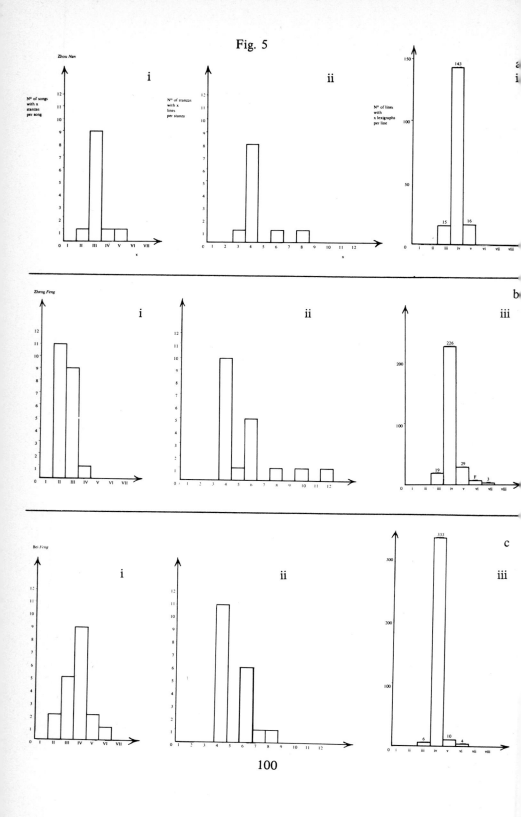

Frequency polygons
a   Zhou Nan
   i   number of songs with x stanzas per song. 75 per cent of the
           population have three stanzas per song.
   ii   numbers of stanzas with x lines per stanza. 73 per cent of the
           population have four lines per stanza.
   iii   numbers of lines with x lexigraphs per line. 82 per cent of the
           population have four lexigraphs per line.

---

b   Zheng Feng
   i   numbers of songs with x stanzas per song.
   ii   numbers of stanzas with x lines per stanza. 94 per cent of the
           population have an even number of lines per stanza.
   iii   numbers of lines with x lexigraphs per line. 80 per cent of the
           population have four lexigraphs per line.

---

c   Bei Feng
   i   numbers of songs with x stanzas per song. 63 per cent of the
           population have an even number of stanzas per song.
   ii   numbers of stanzas with x lines per stanza. 95 per cent of the
           population have an even number of lines per stanza.
   iii   numbers of lines with x lexigraphs per line. 94 per cent of the
           population have four lexigraphs per line.

THE FORMAL DISTINCTIONS BETWEEN THE SONG-REPERTORIES OF DIFFERENT STATES

Common to Zhou Nan, Qi Feng[40], Shao Nan, Yong Feng[41], and Wei Feng[42] is the type falling within type D from the Xiao Ya, a song of three stanzas of four lines of four syllables. Three-stanza forms also occur in the traditions of Chen[43], Bei[44], Wang[45], Zheng[46], Tang, Qin[47], Gui[48], Cao[49] and Wei[50]; but as the structural diagrams and distribution polygons show, some of these traditions are clearly distinguishable from each other on the basis of the distribution curves. The Zhou Nan repertory favours songs with three stanzas; that of Zheng, songs with two stanzas; and that of Bei, songs with four stanzas. Again, while the most common stanza-structure in Zhou Nan is that with four lines to the stanza, the curve for Zheng songs shows peaks at four and six lines/ stanza, as does that for Bei songs. About half the Shao Nan songs are regular, with three stanzas of four lines, while about half are irregular, with three stanzas of three, five, and six lines respectively.

Furthermore, songs may *either* be 'regular' (R) — that is, all stanzas have the same number of lines, and all lines have the same number of lexigraphs to the line; *or* 'isorhythmic' (I) with all stanzas of the same number of lines, and with the number of lexigraphs per line *not* the same, but with the pattern the same for all stanzas — for example, four stanzas, each consisting of lines of four, three, four, and five lexigraphs in that order; each stanza then has the same overall rhythmic structure. Lastly, songs are classed as 'heterorhythmic' (H), if the number of lexigraphs per line varies from stanza to stanza. The most uneventful (and hence the dullest) rhythmic structure is indicated by R; the most varied, by H. If each song is classed as R, I, or H, and if the numbers of these in the repertory of a given state is counted, the ratio: R/I+H) (where I or H may be zero) is a measure of regularity, becoming infinity when both I and H are

40 齊風

41 庸風

42 衞風

43 陳

44 邶

45 王

46 鄭

47 秦

48 檜

49 曹

50 魏

102

zero. Infinite regularity is thus equated with minimal rhythmic variety. The most regular songs are those of Zhou Nan (ratio: 10); the least regular are those of Zheng (ratio: 0.6), Tang (0.4), Qi (0.7), and Wang (0.7) (omitting states represented by fewer than ten songs).

Clearly, the traditions of different states are differentiated (1) by the modes of the distribution polygons: Zhou Nan favours three stanzas of four lines; Zheng favour two stanzas of four lines; and Bei favours four stanzas of four lines. In addition, however, the repertories differ (2) in the degree of irregularity exhibited by the songs. Zheng, over and above a predilection for two stanzas, is characterised by a high degree of irregularity.

THE BINARY, ADDITIVE PRINCIPLE OF RHYTHMIC CONSTRUCTION OF SHI-JING SONG-TEXTS AT THE LEVEL OF SONG- AND STANZA-STRUCTURE

Turning now to the distribution polygons for the earlier Zhou period (text-figures 1b, 2b, 3b), the curves are *polymodal* — that is to say, a number of different forms are favoured — rather than (as are those of the *Guo Feng*) *unimodal*. In the *Xiao Ya* repertory (text-figure 3b), the frequencies of songs of three and four stanzas, and of stanzas of four or six lines, are about equal. The distribution curves also show peaks, however, at six and eight stanzas, and at eight and twelve lines. Evidently, with respect to lines, and to some extent with respect to stanzas, *even* numbers of units are favoured, rather than *odd*.

This suggests a principle of binary construction operating on two time-scales: (a), at the level of stanza-structure, stanzas tending to be lengthened by the addition of units of two lines at a time; and (b), at the level of song-structure, the length of a song tending to be increased by two stanzas at a time.

In the *Da Ya* also, there are maxima in the distribution curves at six and eight stanzas to the song, and at four, six and eight lines to the stanza (text-figure 2b). Again, a process of building by the aggregation of binary units of different time-scales is suggested by the data.

NON-ADDITIVE LINE-BUILDING AND ITS RHYTHMIC IMPLICATIONS

There exists, however, a third time-scale, but one on which the principle of lengthening by the addition of binary units does not operate; namely, that of the individual verse-line. As stated already with regard to the frequency/syllable-number curve for lines from the Zhou *song*, such distribution curves are *unimodal*, with a very large maximum at four syllables to the line (text-figures 1bii, 2biii, 3biii, 5).

The musical implications of such curves as these are important. First, the skew, non-symmetrical character of the curves (with the exception of 5aiii, biii, ciii) shows that the tendency to lengthen the four-syllable line is markedly greater than the tendency to shorten it; secondly, the absence of maxima on even numbers of syllables (apart from 4) means that there is no tendency for the line-structure to be extended by adding binary units consisting of two sub-units of equal duration. Thus the binary principle of construction observed on the two higher time-scales is inoperative at the level of the musical line. The statistical evidence is overwhelmingly against the hypothesis of an additive principle in line-building.

This implies that syllables added to a line do *not* lengthen the line in time. Were the time to be lengthened, the successive odd and even numbers of syllables (as syllables were added) would normally lead to frequency-maxima on even numbers, since in a predominantly binary rhythmic structure, lines of odd numbers of three, five, or seven time-units (beats) will disturb the overall binary rhythm; whereas lines of two, four, and six beats fit into the general rhythmic pattern.

The only possible rhythmic alternative to additive extension of the verse - and musical line is divisive interpolation; that is, the incorporation of extra syllables by halving of time units.

In the light of this conclusion, there can be little doubt that, even at the earliest period — remembering that the Zhou *song* lines show the same unimodal type of distribution curve, with a single maximum (text-figure 1bii) — a four-syllable line was sung to a musical measure of four equal beats, and that additional syllables were incorporated into the line by halving beats. This is what happens today in Bedouin song-tunes, when an extra syllable is interpolated into the octosyllabic, equal-beat verse-line: a beat is halved; for example, two semiquaver-notes replace a quaver-note.[51]

THE GENERAL ARCHITECTONIC PRINCIPLES OF SONG-TEXT CONSTRUCTION

There can scarcely be any direct proof, at this distance in time, that the Shi Jing songs were sung, as postulated here, in common time; but this last-mentioned evidence plainly excludes one possibility, namely, that the rhythmic pattern of the musical line was extended by the addition of units of equal duration. This conclusion is the more striking in that the statistical evidence shows indubitably that the additive principle did function at two higher levels of organisation in time, in the building of stanzas from lines, and to some extent in the building of stanzas into songs. Furthermore, both stanza- and song-structure tended to extend in units formed of two equal parts, namely, binary units. At the lower structural level, this means, that the couplet of (4+4) syllables was frequently (if not always) a musical unit, to be exchanged as such between songs (as suggested by the evidence from line-sharing; see f.n.2). At the

---

[51]   Observation based on tape-recordings made in the field by Mr. Smart. See footnote 17.

higher structural level, the statistical evidence also suggests that stanzas tended to associate in complementary pairs, forming a higher-order musical and semantic unit. It should be emphasized, however, that the frequency-distribution polygons show clearly that, while structures of (n x 2) basic units were preferred, structures of (2n + 1) units were also possible, both at stanza-level and at song-level.

SUGGESTED FORMAL CHARACTERISTICS OF SHI-MELODIES

While a musical line associated with (4+4) syllables was the norm, and presumably implied a melodic curve moving from 'initial' to 'final' or 'sub-final' (whether in medial, initial, or final positions) (see f.n.4), the half-unit could function as a musical half line in final position in the stanza (and possibly elsewhere as well). Again, the musical balance of an entire song was evidently not upset by the presence of an odd number of stanzas.

To these inferences regarding the musical structure of the songs must be added the evidence that melodies of the Shi Jing songs were probably through-composed (*durchkomponiert*). In the melodies preserved by Zhu Xi (see f.n. 4) and by Zhu Zaiyu, text-stanzas are never sung to the same stanza-tune; but the same tune-line may occur in different stanzas, sometimes in the same position, sometimes in a different position, in the stanza. Such internal 'refrains' hold the entire musical structure together.[52] There is some evidence from the texts themselves that through-composed melody existed in ancient times. Particularly striking is the passage[53] in Mao 259 (Waley 137): 'Ji Fu made this *song*; its song-text (shi) is very long (kong-shi), its air (feng) is long and fine' ('long and lovely', Waley; 'extensive and fine', Karlgren[54]) (si hao). These statements seem to indicate the association of a long text with a long melody. If melody had been stanzaic — the same tune serving for all stanzas — the air would not have grown longer as the text was extended. The statement in Mao 259 is therefore compatible with the view that the melody of the songs was not stanzaic; that it was indeed like the tunes preserved by Zhu Xi.

HISTORICAL AND REGIONAL STRUCTURAL DIFFERENTIATION IN SHI JING SONG-TEXTS

Structural analysis of the songs undertaken here makes plain that, even though (as shown by Dobson) dialectal differences had presumably been eliminated, at an early stage in the editing of the text, from songs within the same major sections (Da Ya, Xiao Ya or Guo Feng), the sections are nevertheless distinguishable by the forms of their respective songs. In Qi Feng, furthermore, though no dialectal differences between the traditions of the different states survive, these same traditions are clearly differentiated by the structure of the

---

[52] L.E.R. Picken, 'Chiang K'uei's *Nine Songs for Yueh*', *The Musical Quarterly*, (1957), 43, pp.201-19.

[53] 吉甫作誦，其詩孔碩，其風肆好

[54] Bernhard Karlgren, *The Book of Odes* (Stockholm, 1950).

songs they contain, in respect of (a) preferred number of stanzas, (b) preferred number of lines to the stanza, and (c) regularity or irregularity of the structure of the verse-lines.

SONG-TEXT TYPE AND MUSICAL INTEREST

The last point (c) may throw light on the well-known story from the Li Ji concerning Marquis Wen (426-387 B.C.) of Wei[55]. To the philosopher Zi Xia, the Marquis disclosed that he had great difficulty in keeping awake when listening to the old (ritual) music, but never tired when listening to the tunes/songs/music of Zheng and Wei. Table 1 shows structural features of the repertory of Zhou and South of Zhou — the correct songs.

Zhou Nan   TABLE I

Mao Number	Number of Stanzas	r or i*	lines/ stanza	syllables/ line	R, I** or H
1	V	r	4	iv	R
2	III	r	6	iv	R
3	IV	r	4	iv	R
4	III	r	4	iv	R
5	III	r	4	iv	R
6	III	r	4	iv	R
7	III	r	4	iv	R
8	III	r	4	iv	R
9	III	r	8	iv	R
10	III	r	4	iv	R
11	III	r	3	iii, iv, iv	I

*r   all stanzas have the same number of lines; i, all stanzas do not have the same number of lines;

**R   all lines in the stanza have the same number of syllables;

I   all lines in the stanza do not have the same number of syllables, but the pattern is the same for all stanzas;

H   the number of syllables per line varies from stanza to stanza.

55   四部叢刊，纂圖互註禮記，j. 11，樂記第十九，15a：魏文侯問於子夏曰。吾端冕而聽古樂。則唯恐臥。人。聽鄭衛之音。則不知倦。敢問古樂之如彼何也。新樂之如此何也   . 'Marquis Wen of Wei enquired of Zi Xia, saying: "When in ceremonial robe and cap I listen to the old ritual music, I am simply afraid of falling asleep. But if I listen to the songs/tunes of Zheng and Wei, I know no fatigue. I beg to ask: What is it about the old music that makes it like that? What is it about the new music that makes it like this?" ' For the context of this incident, the reader may refer to S. Couvreur, S.J.; *Li Ki* (1913), vol. ii, pp.44ff., and in particular to pp.49 and 86; also to E. Chavannes, *Les Mémoires historiques de Se-ma Tsien* (1898), vol. iii, pp.238ff., and in particular p.272.

106

With one exception all the songs are completely regular: all stanzas consist of the same number of lines, and all lines consist of the same number of syllables.

Table II displays the repertory of Zheng: a high proportion of the songs are irregular, showing a variety of line-rhythms, of isorhythmic or heterorhythmic type. It may then have been the rhythmic interest of the tunes (yin[56]) of Zheng that kept the Marquis awake; it cannot have been their length, since they were not appreciably shorter than the Zhou Nan. The Zhou Nan and the earlier Ya may have been elevating in effect but, by their very regularity, they will have been conducive (even when combined with dance and spectacle) to sleep.

The song-types A, B, C, and D, as distinguished in this essay, constitute a series of increasing musical complexity and interest, reaching a peak in the sub-type of Zheng, where the greatest irregularity of line is encountered in song-structures of shortest duration. The serial order of Mao approximately reverses this order (see p.90), in accordance with Chinese notions of an order of potency, by which the most venerable occupies the final position in a series.

There can be little doubt that the tunes of Zheng enshrined that formal principle of 'rhythmic diversity within a fixed metrical framework' which is characteristic of all later Chinese song. It is to be noticed that this formal development appears to have occurred first in states remote from peripheral influences, that is, occupying a central position in the complex of states of the Chunqiu period (722-481 B.C.).

A VESTIGE OF THE MUSIC OF ZHOU?

For those hungering for a snatch of *music* in an abstract discussion of *forms,* I would like to suggest that a single cadential line may have survived from Zhou times, preserved by Zhu Xi in the melody for Nan shan you tai[57] (Mao 172). It is the line: Wan shou wu jiang[58], occurring in this song as the final line of Stanza II. The same text-line occurs also in Mao 154, 209 and 211, always in final position in the stanza and mostly as the last line of a song.[3] The exciting fact is: that in Zhu Xi's melody the corresponding musical line is a purely 'pentatonic' fragment, lacking auxiliaries: c d g f. Moreover, this line is, musically regarded, of the most splendidly affirmatory and final character. It fits the intention of the text-line perfectly. It is indeed worthy to be a vestige of the Xiao Ya of Zhou. The same musical phrase with different textual underlays occurs seven times in all in three (Mao 161, 162, 172) of the six huang-zhong qing-gong[59] song-melodies: twice as the end of a stanza, elsewhere as the latter

56 音

57 南 山 有 臺

58 萬 壽 無 疆   : 'A myriad life-spans without limit!'

59 黃 鐘 清 宮

TABLE II

Zheng Feng

Mao Number	Number of stanzas	r or i**	lines/ stanza	syllables/ line	R, I or H**
75	III	r	4	I-III:v,vi,v,vii	I
76	III	r	8	I,II:iv,iv,v,iv, iv,iv,iv,iv	
				III:iv,iv,v,iv, v,iv,iv,iv	H
77	III	r	5	I-III:iii,iv,iv, iv,iv	I
78	III	r	10	I:iv,iii,iv,iv,. iii,iv,iv,iv, iv,iv	
				II:iii,iii,iv,iv, iii,iv,iv,iv,iv,iv	
				III:iii,iii,iv,iv, iii,iv,iv,iv,iv	H
79	III	r	4	I,II:iv,iv,iv,v	
				III:iv,iv,iv,iv	H
80	III	r	4	iv	R
81	II	r	4	I,II:iv,vi,iv,iv	I
82	III	r	6	I,II:iv,iv,iv,iv, iv,iv	
				III:v,v,v,v,v,v	H
83	II	r	6	iv	R
84	II	r	4	iv	R
85	II	r	4	iv	R
86	II	r	4	I,II:iv,v,iv,vi	I
87	II	r	5	I,II:iv,iv,iv,iv,vi	I
88	IV	i	3,3,4,4	I,II:iv,v,v	
				III,IV:iv,iv,iv,iv	H
89	II	r	4	iv	R
90	III	r	4	iv	R
91	III	r	4	I:iv,iv,iv,v	
				II,III:iv,iv,iv,iv	H
92	II	r	6	I,II:iii,iv,iv,iv v.iv	I
93	II	r	6	iv	R
94	II	r	6	iv	R
95	II	r	12	I,II:iii,iv,iii, iv,iv,iv,iv,iii, iv,iv,iv,v	H

of a pair of musical lines, in medial position. Evidently, it always carried some degree of musical finality — for Chinese ears, as for ours.

Finally, lest it be felt that the discussion of songs in the absence of any surviving melodies is a sterile exercise, it must be emphasized that the fundamental and most distinctive characteristics of a music are neither modal nor rhythmic (on a small time-scale) but formal. As Sachs[60] clearly recognized, form and rhythm are overlapping concepts; and it is in accordance with this general principle that a tendency to binary organization manifests itself at so many different levels in the structure of the Shi Jing songs.

Acknowledgements

It is a pleasure to acknowledge my varied debts to several friends; firstly, to Mr. Wyn Guneratne, B.A., formerly of St. Catharine's College, Cambridge, who first showed me how to calculate the number of different musical lines possible, using a fixed number of notes, four at a time; secondly, to Dr. Trevor Page, of Jesus College, Cambridge, who read and made most helpful comments on the text and re-drew all my text-figures and histograms; and lastly, to Mr. Jeremy Rudge, of Jesus College, who discussed with me statistical aspects of the data assembled.

[60]   Curt Sachs, *The Wellsprings of Music* (1965).

A ninth-century Sino-Japanese lute-tutor

R.F. WOLPERT

(Peterhouse, Cambridge)

DESCRIPTION OF THE MANUSCRIPT

This preliminary study includes an annotated translation of preface and colophon, a transcription of all modal preludes, together with an explanation of the twenty-eight tunings, in the manuscript from the Fushiminomiya collection (now housed in Kunaichō Shoryōbu) known as the 'Book of Lute Tablatures of the Fushiminomiya Family *Fushiminomiya-bon Biwa-fu*[a]', henceforth FBBF.

I have worked from the superb facsimile of this manuscript (prepared under the auspices of Kunaichō Shoryōbu), a copy of which was generously presented to the University Library, Cambridge, in 1972, by the Grand Steward of the Imperial Household[1].

The FBBF is a tenth-century copy of an original manuscript written in A.D. 838 by Lian Chengwu[b] of Yangchow for his pupil Fujiwara Sadatoshi[c], an Assistant Officer in a Japanese mission. This mission left for China in 834/5 and arrived at Yangchow in the tenth month of 838.

The FBBF is a scroll composed of twenty-five sheets of paper glued together in sequence. The sheet-size is 230 x 273 mm. The first and last sheets are of a different size, namely 230 x 220 mm. Differently tinted papers, sprinkled with silver and gold foil, were used in assembling the scroll[2]. A coloured backing paper was removed in Edo-times and replaced by plain white paper. The upper and lower margins are 27 mm from the top and bottom of the sheets. Each sheet is ruled with twelve lines in silver paint, except the first, which has eleven lines. A sheet is missing between the present sheets ten and eleven [3].

---

[1] University Library, Cambridge; now catalogued as FH.990 32. (and wrongly attributed to Liu Erh-lang (sic)).

[2] 'Cloud paper' 雲紙 ; see Nihon-no kami 日本の紙 , Nihon-no rekishi sōsho 14 日本歴史叢書 , Tokyo, 1968.

[3] See the pamphlet accompanying the facsimile reproduction of FBBF, Fushiminomiya-bon biwa-fu kaidai 伏見宮本琵琶譜解題, p. 1. The fact that a sheet is missing is obvious from the musical context; see p.162.

(a) 伏見宮本琵琶譜   (b) 廉承武   (c) 藤原貞敏

111

The contents of the manuscript fall into four major sections:

1) A preface, in part copied from the original, and in part composed by the copyist and teacher (Sadayasu Shinnō[d]) of the addressee.

2) Modal preludes[4]
'Fourteen modal preludes[5]
Fengxiang tiao (four)/Fan Fengxiang tiao (four)/Huangzhong tiao (four)/[Right-] Hand-fingered huangzhong [tiao] (two)/Fan Huangzhong tiao, modal prelude in the *lü*-tone (two)/Qing tiao and Fan Qing tiao tuning etc./Rules for the use of the hand/Rules for modal tuning/Notes on tablature [signs]'.

3) Tunings and short tuning pieces (*xianhe**) for twenty-seven (out of a theoretical total of twenty-eight) modes.

4) A colophon, originally dated and signed by Fujiwara Sadatoshi.

This paper does not follow the order of FBBF, but deals with the contents of the manuscript in a rearranged order. Since FBBF is a copy of a Chinese manuscript, all transcriptions of modal names, etc., are into Chinese rather than Sino-Japanese. For convenience, names of degrees of the scale are shown in Chinese and Sino-Japanese readings; for example: bianzhi/hen-chi. For tablature signs (for flute and for biwa) only Sino-Japanese readings are given, since the Chinese readings are not known with certainty.

TABLATURE

The tuning of the lute piba/biwa[e] is shown in various ways in different manuscripts. Open (unstopped) strings are equated with a stopped (fingered) note at the same pitch (or at the octave). Because the spacing of the frets on the neck of the Sino-Japanese lute is constant, a relative tuning of the four open strings of any piba/biwa can be established by this procedure. The absolute pitch is fixed by tuning one of the open strings to a note on a wind-instrument, normally the flute di/teki[f]. In order to relate the tablature signs to their abstract equivalents in the *lü*-scale[6] they are shown both in relative pitches and in relationship to the 'concert pitch' huangzhong[g] in the absolute system.

---

[4] There follows a translation of the Table of Contents, FBBF sheet 2, lines 9 ff and sheet 3, line 1. It is not proposed on this occasion to attempt a translation of Chinese modal names.

[5] Of the sixteen pieces listed in the Table of Contents (in the heading erroneously stated to be fourteen), thirteen are fully preserved, one is preserved in part, and two seem to be missing.

[6] See L. E. R. Picken, 'The Music of Far Eastern Asia: 1. China', *The New Oxford History of Music* I (London 1957), pp. 94-6.

(d) 貞保新王   (e) 琵琶   (f) 笛   * p. 123

112

The oldest known piba/biwa tablatures are the *Tempyō biwa-fu*[7], henceforth Tempyō, dated about 738; the FBBF; the two piba tablatures preserved in the Collection Pelliot from Dunhuang[8], henceforth P.3808 and P.3539; and the early Japanese biwa manuscript, Sango-yōroku[9], henceforth SGYR. The main symbols of the tablature used in all these manuscripts have been preserved unchanged in the partbooks of Japanese court music[10].

The tablature consists of twenty primary symbols unambiguously showing the finger or fret position on the four strings.

TEMPYŌ   一 乚 扌 𠄌 〇 ス 乚 八 几 十 乚 〇 〇 〇 〇 𠆢 ㄓ 〇 〇 ㄨ

FBBF   一 乚 夕 𠄌 エ 下 七 八 九 十 匕 丨 フ 乚 乀 厶 斗 工 乙 也

P3539   一 乚 𠂊 上 ユ ス 土 八 九 十 匕 乚 フ 乚 丨 玄 丿 乀 乙 匕

P3808   一 乚 夕 𠄌 ユ ス 七 八 几 十 匕 丨 フ 丶 乀 厶 斗 乀 ㄨ

SGYR   一 乚 夕 𠄌 ユ 下 七 八 九 十 匕 丨 フ 乚 乀 厶 斗 工 乙 也

---

[7] Hayashi Kenzō 林謙三 , Tempyō biwa-fu 'bankasū' no kaisetsu 天平琵琶譜「番仮崇」の解読 , *Gagaku* 雅樂 (Tokyo 1969), pp. 124-37; a photographic reproduction of this fragment is to be found in Kishibe Shigeo 岸边成雄 , et. al., Shōsōin-no gakki 正倉の樂器 (Tokyo 1967), plate 119.

[8] Undated manuscripts; facsimile reproductions in 'Airs de Touen houang', *Mission Paul Pelliot* II (Paris 1971), plates 54-57 (P. 3808), and plate 58 (P. 3539). Secondary material is discussed by P.Demiéville in the introduction, pp. 33-4.

[9] By Fujiwara Moronaga 藤原師長 , 1137-92; the original manuscript is to be dated between 1171 and 1192. The copy used was written in 1328, and is stated to be a copy of a copy made in 1208.

[10] This contradicts D. P. Berger's general statement, that tablatures imported from China were changed in Japan. See D. P. Berger, 'The Shakuhachi and the Kinko Ryū Notation', *Asian Music* I,2 (New York 1969), p. 33.

(g) 黃鐘

113

In FBBF, P.3539 and SGYR the definitions of the tablature signs for piba/biwa lead to the following scheme: (Roman numerals designate strings; arabic numerals, frets.)[11]

	IV	III	II	I	
	一	凵	勺	丄	
0	ichi	otsu	gyō	jō	Open string
	工	下	七	八	
1	ku	ge	shichi	hachi	1st fret
	几	十	ヒ	丨	
2	bō	jū	ni	boku	2nd fret
	刁	乙	乚	厶	
3	shū	bi	gon	sen	3rd fret
	斗	乛	之	也	
4	tō	ko	shi	ya	4th fret

Since piba from the Tang period[12] are preserved in the Shōsōin at Nara, the exact dimensions of the spaces between the frets are known[13]; these are identical with those on the gaku-biwa[h] used in modern Tōgaku[14] performance.

The Tang piba, like its modern successor the gaku-biwa, had four strings and four frets, allowing the player a range of five notes on each string. The intervals resulting from the positions of the frets on the neck are

      between Open String and First Fret   ---- tone
      between First Fret and Second Fret   ---- semitone
      between Second Fret and Third Fret   ---- semitone
      between Third Fret and Fourth Fret   ---- semitone

Absolute pitch is expressed in relation to the Chinese 'concert pitch' huangzhong.

The instrument may be tuned in a variety of ways. Frequently a change in tuning-procedure seems to be undertaken in order to enable a wind instrument to play the tune in a given mode. This results only in a change of pitch, not in a change in the size of the intervals between the open strings.

The following are the instructions for tuning given in FBBF[15], together with the corresponding instructions in SGYR, where applicable. Tuning-procedures will be demonstrated by diagrams (in addition to the

[11]   FBBF sheet 15, lines 2-4; SGYR maki 1, lines 4-8.

[12]   Tang dynasty 618-906.

[13]   Shōsōin no gakki, p. 82.

[14]   Tōgaku 唐樂, 'music of Tang', a part of Japanese court music.

[15]   FBBF sheet 14, lines 2-6.

(h)   樂琵琶

translations) similar to that already used in setting out the relationships between frets, and tablature signs. In these diagrams, the sign $\supset$ placed to the right, indicates a step of a tone between frets; $>$ indicates a semitone. Interspersed textual passages are translated as they occur in FBBF.

TUNINGS FOR FOUR PRINCIPAL MODES

'Tiaozi pin[16]
Fengxiang tiao
Match [literally: 'make congruent', 'harmonize'] the notes using IV_0: IV_0

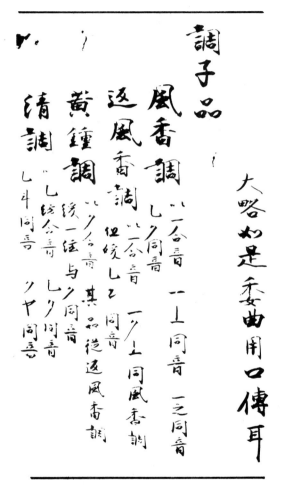

Plate 1a: Instructions for the four principal tunings

[16]   Tiaozi pin 調 子 品 : 'the frets in a mode'. Tiaozi pin is the general name for tuning instructions in FBBF.

and I_0 are the same note [that is, apart from the octave difference]; IV_0 and II_4 are the same note; III_3 and II_0 are the same note.'

In defining tunings in the four principal modes, FBBF does not equate string pitches with flute pitches (though such equations are given in defining the 27 modes). Flute pitches are given, however, in SGYR.

The following is a translation of the instructions for the corresponding tuning in SGYR[17],:

'Fengxiang tiao

Match the notes using IV_0 (flute in Huang, a-hole; in Ban, b-hole[18])[19].
IV_0 and I_0 are the same note [that is, apart from the octave difference]; match I_0 with II_0 (flute in Huang, e; in Ban, f$^\sharp$). I_0 and II_4 are the same note; match II_0 with III_0 (Huang, c; Ban, d), II_0 and III_3 are the same note.'

These instructions result in the following alternative tunings for the lute in Fengxiang tiao:

Flute in Huangzhong tiao	A*	c	e	a
Flute in Banshi tiao	B	d	f	b
	IV_0	III_0	II_0	I_0

and define all tablature signs in Fengxiang tiao as follows (flute in Huangzhong tiao as standard):

[17]   SGYR maki 2, lines 22 ff.

[18]   b is here b$\natural$ as in English usage, not b$\flat$, as in German usage!

[19]   For a discussion of Tang modes, see M. Gimm, Das Yüeh-fu tsa-lu des Tuan An-chieh, Studien zur Geschichte von Musik, Schauspiel und Tanz in der T'ang Dynastie, *Asiatische Forschungen* 19, (Wiesbaden 1966), pp. 543-67; L. E. R. Picken, T'ang Music and Musical Instruments, *T'oung Pao*, Vol. 55 (Leiden 1969), pp. 92-100.

In its account of the Japanese modal structure of Fengxiang tiao, **SGYR** further confirms the appropriateness of this tuning for the specified mode, by relating fret-positions to the notes of the basic diatonic scale. In (a) (below), for example, the initial of the basic series: gong/kyū ($\equiv$ do) can be obtained at three fret positions as shown.

gong/kyū			一	丄	(a)
shang/shō	工			𠆢丶	(b)
jue/kaku	𠃌	㇄		⎮	(c)
bianzhi/hen-chi	扌	下		㐄	(d)
zhi/chi		乙	㇉		(e)
yu/u			七		(♯)
biangong/hen-kyū			𠃊		(g)

FBBF continues:

'Fan Fengxiang tiao
Match the notes using IV'_0; IV_0, II_0 and I_0 are the same as in Fengxiang tiao; re-tuning III_0, it is the same as IV_1.'

This tuning also is confirmed by SGYR[20]:

'Fan·Fengxiang tiao
(Corresponds to Shuang tiao and Shui tiao on di/teki).
Match the notes using IV_0 (flute in Shuang, g; in Shui, a); IV_0 and I_0 are the same note [apart from the octave difference]; as to the correspondence between I_0 and II_0 (flute in Shuang, d; in Shui, e), I_0 and II_4 are the same note; as to the correspondence between II_0 and III_0 (flute in Shuang, a; in Shui, b), II_0 and III_4 are the same note; III_0 and I_1 are the same note.
Secret note; Fan Fengxiang tiao. IV_0, II_4 and I_0 are gong/kyū [henceforth *do*]. IV_1, III_0 and I_1 are shang/shō [henceforth *re*]. IV_3, III_1 and I_3 are jue/kaku [henceforth *mi*]. III_3 is bianzhi/hen-chi [henceforth *fa*]. III_4 and II_0 are zhi/chi [henceforth *so*]. II_1 is yu/u [henceforth *la*]. II_3 is biangong/hen-kyū [henceforth *si*].'

Accordingly the alternative tunings in Fan Fengxiang tiao are:

	IV_0	III_0	II_0	I_0
Flute in Shuang tiao	G	A	d	g
Flute in Shui tiao	A	B	e	a

[20] SGYR maki 2, lines 118 ff.

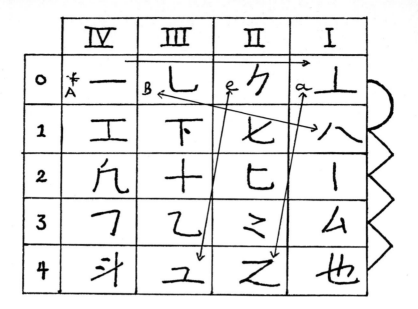

FBBF continues:

'Huangzhong tiao

'Match the notes using II_0; the tuning follows Fan Fengxiang tiao, lowering IV_0 to the same note as II_0 [apart from the octave difference].'

	IV	III	II	I
0	E 一	(B) し	※ e ク	(a) 亠
1	工	下	乇	八
2	仈	十	乚	丨
3	㇆	乙	彡	厶
4	斗	ㄐ	乁	也

SGYR[21] states:

'Huangzhong tiao
(Corresponds to di/teki Ping tiao and Xing tiao.)
Match the notes using II_0 (flute, e), II_0 and IV_0 are the same note [apart from the octave difference]; as to the relationship between II_0 and III_0 (flute, b) II_0 and III_4 are the same note; as to the relationship between II_0 and I_0 (flute, a), III_0 and I_1 are the same note [apart from the octave difference].
Secret note: Huangzhong tiao. IV_0, III_4 and II_0 are *do*. IV_1 and II_1 are *re*. IV_2 and II_2 are *mi*. IV_4 and II_4 and I_0 are *fa*. III_0 and I_1 are *so*. III_1 and I_3 are *la*. III_2 and I_4 are *si*.'

The instructions for Huangzhong tiao tuning result, both for FBBF and SGYR, in

IV_0	III_0	II_0	I_0
E	B	e	a

FBBF continues:

'Qing tiao
Match the notes using III_0; III_0 and II_0 are the same note; III_0 and IV_4 are the same note; II_0 and I_4 are the same note [apart from the octave difference]'.

21   SGYR maki 2, lines 242 ff.

And in SGYR[22] the instructions are:

'Qing tiao

(Corresponds to di/teki Ping tiao and Banshi tiao).

Match the notes using III_0 (flute in Ping[tiao], e; in Ban[-shi tiao], b); III_0 and II_0 are the same note; as to the relationship between III_0 and IV_0 (flute in Ping[-tiao], b; in Ban[-shi tiao], c), III_0 and IV_4 are the same note; IV_0 and I_0 are the same note [apart from the octave difference]; III_0 and I_4 are the same note [apart from the octave difference].'

Secret note; Qing tiao. IV_4, III_0, III_0 and I_4 are *do*. III_1 and II_1 are *re*. III_2 and II_2 are *mi*. III_4 and II_4 are *fa*. IVO and IO are *so*. IV_1 and I_1 are *la*. IV_2 and I_2 are *si*.'

Accordingly the tunings for the lute in Qing taio are:

	IV_0	III_0	II_0	I_0
Flute in Ping tiao	B	e	e	b
Flute in Banshi tiao	F	B	B	f

FBBF continues:

'The number of modal tunings for piba is very great and one cannot carelessly play [through] them. Nevertheless, Sadatoshi easily played all modes. There was nothing we did not work through, but some of his notes were neither good nor bad, and some were not in tune with the flute. The four modes still prepare for the Refined Music[23] (that is, these four modal

---

22 SGYR maki 2, lines 312 ff.

23 Compare with SGYR, maki 2, lines 2ff.

preludes.). The old Vice-governor of Mutsu province [?Fujiwara] Yoshiharu was said to be the transmitter [of the tradition]. If you wish to know a great deal about all of the modal preludes, using the tablature can help you; but not unless you have grasped what your teacher taught you.'[24]

In the following 'Rules for the Tablature', FBBF explains the primary and secondary tablature signs. In addition to the fret-names (the primary tablature signs already explained above, p. 113), a considerable number of secondary signs are used. The functions of some of these have already been described in studies by Hayashi Kenzō[25], L. E. R. Picken[26], and E. Harich-Schneider[27].

SECONDARY TABLATURE SIGNS

The secondary tablature signs in piba/biwa manuscripts may conveniently be divided into two groups, one comprising the instructions for the use of the right hand, that is, for plucking the strings, the other comprising the terms indicating rests, duration, repeats, and sections. Instructions on how to perform the secondary tablature signs in the first group are to be found only in FBBF, but some of these are also used in Tempyo[7].

Technical instructions for the use of the fingers of the right hand[28]:

凵〕 'strike strings as a chord with the thumb, from the lowest to the highest 七〕 indicated string, using the *gou* 勹 movement[29]'

工 'dot on top: index finger'

工 'dot below: thumb'

---

[24]   FBBF sheet 2, lines 5 ff.

[25]   Hayashi Kenzō, 'Study on explication of ancient musical score of P'i-p'a discovered at Tun-huang, China', *Bulletin*, Nara Gakugei University, V,(1955), pp. 1-22; 'On ancient musical score of P'i-p'a discovered at Tun-huang', *Proceedings of the Japan Academy*, XXXII (1956), pp. 451-454; 'Dunhuang piba pu-di jiedu yanjiu 敦煌 琵 琶 譜 的 解 讀 研 究 ', Chinese translation by Pan Huaisu (Shanghai 1957).

[26]   L. E. R. Picken, 'Some Chinese terms for musical repeats, sections and forms common to T'ang, Yüan and Tōgaku scores', *Bulletin of the School of Oriental and African Studies* XXXIV,1 (London 1971), pp. 113-118.

[27]   Eta Harich-Schneider, 'A History of Japanese Music', (London 1973), p. 212.

[28]   Only secondary signs (not as yet, or incorrectly, described, in one or other of the studies [25],[26],[27]) are listed here.

[29]   Plucking the string with the flesh of the finger-tip (or the ball of the thumb); compare R. H. van Gulik's description of qin 琴 technique in his 'The Lore of the Chinese Lute', (Tokyo 1940), p. 127.

工 'without dot: middle finger'

工: 'dot on the right: use the *tiao* 挑 movement[30]'

工 small tablature signs (as in a commentary): 'complete phrase with a *gou* movement of the finger:' (this also indicates 'quavers' in a piece otherwise written in 'crotchets').

二了 'small signs and *liao* 了 : complete plucking movement with the same finger' (that is, inwards-outwards, or outwards-inwards).

力 character *li* 力 'strong': 'thumb and index finger pluck simultaneously' (*forte*).

Terms for rests and durations[28]:

了 'small pause'

火 'pluck fast' (that is, crotchet halved to quaver).

引 'prolong note' (that is, crotchet doubled to minim).

The secondary tablature-signs of the first group are of particular importance. The hitherto accepted view that the Japanese had no knowledge of the right-hand finger-technique common in China in the latter half of the Tang dynasty, and praised in numerous poems[31], has to be revised. Further study of the technical instructions for the use of the right hand in the preliminary list shown above, and of their relationship to literary evidence in contemporary writings, is a task for the future.

MODAL TUNING PIECES AND TUNINGS FOR 27 (28) MODE-KEYS

The tuning instructions for the following twenty-seven (out of twenty-eight) modes for piba, preserved in FBBF, mainly follow the tuning instructions given for the four modes, listed separately and previously explained (above p. 115 ff.). Most tuning instructions are followed by a short 'tuning piece' (*xianhe*), used to check the tuning of the strings, as well as to give the player 'the feel' of a mode. The results of the twenty-seven tuning instructions are shown in the table on p. 132 . The corresponding short tuning-pieces are:

1) Yiyue tiao* (See Plate 1b.)

30 Plucking the string outwards with the nail. See R. H. van Gulik, *loc.cit.*

31 See M. Gimm, *op.cit.*, pp. 346 ff.

*Chinese characters for all mode-key names can be found in Hayashi Kenzō, loc.cit[33].

Plate 1b:
Yiyue tiao, Tuning piece
(FBBF Sheet 16, lines 1-3).

2) Yiyue shang tiao

3) Shashi [or Shato] tiao

*may be B below.

123

4) Shuang tiao

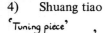

5) Ping tiao

6) Dashi tiao

7) Qishi tiao
'There is no tuning piece included in this score.'

8) Xiaoshi tiao
'There is no tuning piece included in this score.'

9) Dao tiao

10) Huangzhong tiao

11) Da Hoangzhong tiao
III_0, and II_0 and I_0 are from Ping tiao; matching II_3, I_0 is the same note as the IV_0 string [apart from the octave difference].'

The tuning instructions for this mode are mutually contradictory: nevertheless it is possible to establish two different tunings:

Taking the statement regarding the three highest strings together with the information that II_3 is the same note as IV_0, the tuning would be G   B e a.

32 'Arpeggiato is indicated by an elongated hook with the longer side running alongside the sequence of tablature signs.

124

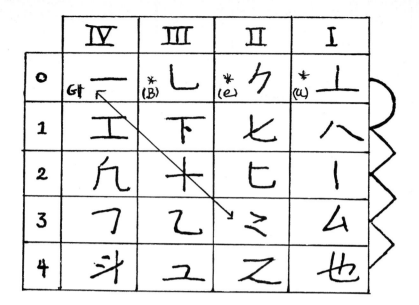

	IV	III	II	I
0	G‡ 一	*(B) し	*(e) ク	*(a) 丄
1	工	下	七	八
2	几	十	匕	丨
3	フ	乙	之	ム
4	斗	工	之	也

Accepting the second statement as correct, and using only the non-conflicting information from the first equation, the tuning would be A B e a.

	IV	III	II	I
0	A 一	*(B) し	*(e) ク	*(a) 丄
1	工	下	七	八
2	几	十	匕	丨
3	フ	乙	之	ム
4	斗	工	之	也

With the two possible tunings the tuning-piece is:

tuning (a) is preferred

12) Shui tiao

'IV_0 and III_4 are the same note [apart from the octave difference]; I_0 and II_1 are the same note; III_0 and I_4 are the same note [apart from the octave difference]; I_0 and II_3 are the same note.'

Again, the instructions for tuning are self-contradictory. If the statement that I_0 and III_3 are the same note is ignored, the tuning is G d g a. If the statement that I_0 and II, are the same note is ignored, the tuning becomes G d f a.

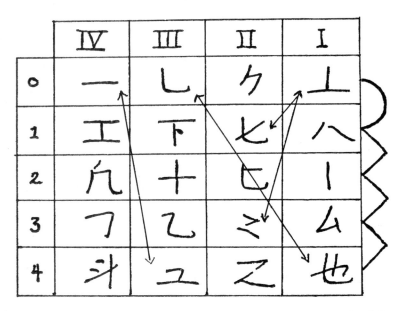

The tuning-piece resulting from the two possible tunings assumes the following forms; tuning (b) is preferred.

*a shake

126

13) Wanshi tiao

14) Fengxiang tiao

15) Fan Fengxiang tiao

16) Xiannü tiao

'II_0 and II_1 are the same note. IV_4 and I_0 are the same note [apart from the octave difference], IV_0 and III_4 are the same note [apart from the octave difference], II_0 and I_4 are the same note [apart from the octave difference], III_0 and I_1 are the same note [apart from the octave difference].'

The first statement: 'II_0 and II_1 are the same note' demands the impossible: the open string cannot produce the same note as the first fret on the same string. This statement must be ignored in attempting to tune the strings in relation to each other. It may, however, indicate a change in absolute pitch, requiring re-tuning of the II_0 string to the note originally produced at the first fret; that is, re-tuning the II_0 string a tone higher.

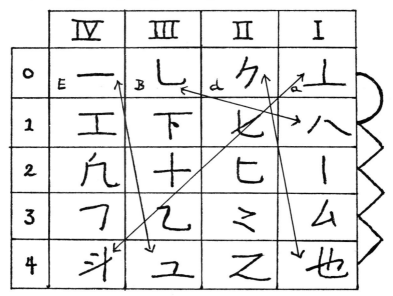

17) Linzhong tiao

* Bb in original — probably copyist's mistake.

18) Qing tiao

19) Shagong tiao

20) No tiao

21) Xianhao tiao

22) According to Hayashi Kenzō[33] the 22nd tuning should be Gaoxian tiao. He assumes that the tuning for this mode is E B e b. However, this mode is *not* named in FBBF, which in fact gives tuning instructions for 27 only of the 28 modes for piba. It will be convenient to number this mode as 22, inspite of the fact that it is not represented in FBBF.

---

[33] Hayashi Kenzō, 'Biwa chōgen-no shuju-sō 琵琶調絃の種種

相 ', *Gagaku* (Tokyo 1969), p. 270.

128

23) Fenghuang tiao
   'Following Biyü tiao. Lower the highest string.'
   Tuning probably B A e g.

24) Yuanyang tiao

25) Nanpin tiao

26) Yushen tiao

27) Biyü tiao
   'IV$_2$ and I$_4$ are the same note [apart from the octave difference], III$_0$ and
   II$_4$ are the same note [apart from the octave difference].'
   The tuning instructions given for Biyü tiao lack a third instruction linking
inner and outer strings.

Tuning-piece resulting from five possible tunings:

In the light of these results, tunings (a) and (e) appear to be unlikely possibilities; tunings (b), (c) and (d) are possible, but tuning (b) affords the most satisfactory solution.

28) Zhuomu tiao
No tuning piece for this mode is included in the score.

The results of this examination of tunings and tuning-pieces are summarized in the following table:[34]

---

[34]   Chinese characters for the mode-key names can be found in Hayashi Kenzō, loc.cit[33].

	1	2	3	4	5	6	7	8	9	10	11	12	13	14	15
Name of mode	Yiyne tiao	Yiyne shang tiao	Shato tiao	Shuang tiao	Ping tiao[35]	Dashi tiao	Qishi tiao	Xiaoshi tiao	Dao tiao	Huangzhong tiao	Da Huangzhong tiao	Shui tiao[36]	Wanshi tiao	Fengxiang tiao	Fan Fengxiang tiao
Tuning IV	F	F	F	A	f#f# F#	f# F#	F#	F#	B	E	G	G G	F#	A	A
III	B	B	B	d	B B	B	B	B	B	B	B	d d	B	c	B
II	e	f#	e	e	e e	e	e	e	g	e	e	g f	e	e	e
I	a	c#	a	a	b a	a	a	a	b	a	a	a a	a	a	a
Corresponding mode-key on flute				Yiyne tiao	Banshi tiao										
Final	a	b	a	d	b	b			b	e	e		f#	a	a
Name of mode-key in tuning instruction in SGYR	Ping tiao		Ping tiao	Shuang tiao	Ping tiao	Ping tiao	Ping tiao	Ping tiao		Huangzhong tiao				Fengxiang tiao	Fan Fengxiang tiao

35   An older tuning, mentioned in FBBF, is shown in smaller type.

36   The second tuning yields a musically satisfactory version of the tuning-piece.

131

		16	17	18	19	20	21	22	23	24	25	26	27	28
Name of mode		Xiannü tiao	Linzhong tiao	Qing tiao	Shagong tiao	No tiao	Xianhao tiao	Gaoxian tiao[37]	Fenghuang tiao	Yuanyang tiao	Nanpin tiao	Yushou tiao	Biyu tiao[38]	Zhuomu tiao
Tuning	IV	E	G#	F#	F#	F#	E		(?)B	F#	A	A	(B) B B	A
	III	B	d	B	B	B	B		A	B	c	c#	(A) d c	A
	II	d	e	B	e	c	e		e	c#	e	e	(e) a g	e
	I	a	b	f#	g#	g#	b		g	f#	e	a	(a) a a	a
Corresponding mode-key on flute										Shuang tiao				
Final		e	e	b	f#	c#	b			b	a	c#	d	
Name of mode-key in tuning instruction in SGYR				Qing tiao						Fengxiang tiao				Zhuomu tiao

37   Hayashi Kenzō suggests Gaoxian tiao as the 22nd mode; his tuning is E B e b.

38   All possible tunings that make musical sense of the tuning piece are given. The most probable tuning is shown ringed.

PREFACE (See Plates 2 and 3)

Piba[39] Tablatures[40]: Preface

Piba-playing is 'horseback-music'[41]. The body [of the piba] exemplifies the Three Powers[42], the strings represent the Four Seasons[43]. They passed the goblet[44] in the years of the Qin[45], they performed subtle melodies in the days of the Han[46]. When the Princess went to the Wusun[47], it eased her grief at

[39] From about the end of the *Sui* dynasty (581-618) onwards, piba was used for the four-stringed, short-necked lute with a pear-shaped body[a]. *

* Secondary footnotes are given on pp. 139-145.

[40] The Chinese term *pu*[a] means musical notations. In most cases it refers to tablatures, that is to notations in which the signs indicate the method of playing – which finger does what, without specifying, neither relatively nor absolutely, the pitch of the notes played. In modern Chinese *pu* stands for any score[b].

[41] *Mashang yue*[a] suggests the music of the Central Asian steppes, whence the lute was introduced into China. In *Jiu Tangshu*[b], it is said of *mashang yue*:
[The music] of the Northern Barbarians, in the three states of *Xianbi*[c], *Tuyuhun*[d], and *Buloji*[e] is all horseback-music.

[42] According to the *Yijing*[a] the Three Powers are: Heaven[b], Earth[c] and Man[d]. In the *Fengsu tongyi*[e] it is said:
The piba is three feet and five inches long. Three and Five resemble the Three Powers: Heaven, Earth, and Man, and the Five Elements[f].

[43] *Sishi*[a]. The association of the lute with the Chinese cosmological system fits an originally non-Chinese musical instrument into the purely Chinese speculative system. At the same time allusions serve to make the foreign instrument respectable. It was never introduced into Chinese ritual music and always remained an instrument of secular music.

[44] This passage points to the 'Poetical Essay on the Lute'[a] by Yu Shinan[b]:
Vigorous was its beginning in the times of the Qin[c]; flooding to full depth, it expanded at the times of the Han[d].

[45] *Qin* dynasty 221-207 B.C.[44c]. This passage suggests the 'Poetical Essay on the Lute' by Fu Xuan[a]:
According to Du Zhi[b] at the end of the Qin dynasty the masses of forced-labour who had to build the Great Wall strung drums with strings.[c]

[46] *Han* dynasty 206 BC - AD 220[44d].

[47] Chinese sources suggest that the *Wusun*[a] were blue-eyed and red-haired herdsmen, who lived in the region of the Tianshan[b] range around lake Issik-köl[c].

133

separation[48]. As Zhaojun left the Imperial Palace, it brought comfort in her sorrow at marrying far away[49]. At Golden-valley[50] as he trifled with flowers, Shi Jilun[51] played this [the lute] to give him pleasure. At Bamboo-grove[52] as he pledged in wine[53], Ruan Zhongyong[54] played it to express his feelings[55].

[48]   The historical background to which this passage refers, is the alliance-policy of the *Han*-emperor Wudi[a], following the successful second mission of his general Chang Qian[b] to the *Wusun*[47]. The *Wusun* joined in an alliance with the Chinese against the *Xiongnu*[c].

        In the period Yuanfeng[d] the Princess Xijun[e], daughter of Prince Jian of Jiangdu[f] was sent as a wife to the *Wusun* . . .and Kunmo[g] made her his Wife of the Right. . . .The Princess wrote the poem 'My family gave me in marriage[h].[i]

Later the Princess became the wife of Kunmo's grandson[j]. After the king's death the Princess submitted a memorial asking leave to return to China[k]. She died in China in 49 BC.

The first association of the Princess Xijun (popularly known as the Wusun-Princess) with the piba occurs in the 'Poetical Essay on the Lute' by Fu Xuan[45][a],[c]. No known official record makes this link. Later sources suggest that the Princess invented the piba. This is a further attempt to provide the instrument with a 'proper', that is, a Chinese inventor[l].

[49]   The story of the Princess *Wang Zhaojun*[a], a lady in the harem of the Han Emperor Yuandi[b] and her connection with the lute is told in the preface to Shi Chong's[51] poem: Wangming junci[c]:

        Wang Mingjun's original name was Wang Zhaojun; I have changed this name, because the character Zhao occurs in the name of [Jin] Wendi[d]. When the Xiongnu were powerful, their leader asked for the hand of a Chinese princess in marriage. Emperor Yuandi gave him as wife a girl of good family from his own harem, by name Zhaojun. In former times an Imperial Princess had married the king of the Wusun. The Emperor caused songs to be played on the lute to hearten her as she departed. When Mingjun set out it must have been similar. I have noted down a song, which was written then and which is especially sad.[e]

Both Shi Chong's and Fu Xuan's poems refer to an older anecdote in *Xijing Zaji*[f] on *Wang Qiang*[g].

The popularity of this theme can be seen from the fact that the Yuan opera on the subject of Wang Zhaojun is listed first in the collection of Yuan pieces[h]. The *Tōgaku*[i] repertory includes a piece entitled *Ōshōkun* ≡ Wang Zhaojun[j]. A piece of the same name is to be found in the ninth-century score for five-stringed lute[k].

[50]   The first character in Golden-valley[a] is illegible, and the second character is an alternative reading[b]. Anecdotes relating to Shi Chong and life on his estate, *Jingu yuan*[c], on the borders of Honan, are to be found in *Shishuo xinyu*[d].

[51]   *Shi Chong*[a] was the wealthiest man of his time. In addition to being one of the great poets and scholars of the Jin[b], he sponsored the arts, especially music[c], and was himself an outstanding lute player.[d]

[52]   The first character in Bamboo-grove[a] has partly been destroyed by a bookworm[b]. Ruan Xian[54] was one of the 'Seven Sages of the Bamboo-grove'[c].

[53]   As the poet Liu Ling[a], another member of the group of the 'Seven Sages of the Bamboo-grove' was well known as a wine-bibber[b], so was Ruan Xian[c].

[54]   *Ruan Xian*[a] was the nephew of the scholar Ruan Ji[b], and one of the most famous musicians of his time. According to his biography,

        Xian was well versed in musical theory[c] and played the piba well.[d]

134

With this instrument, Dajō hō'ō[56] established the mean between the hasty and the leisurely, and regulated the balance between diffuse and dense.

By Imperial Order Kōzuke no Taishu Shinnō[57] then came to me to study these melodies[58]. In my humble opinion: things that are secret are to be prized, therefore one must await those who understand the worth of what is deeply stored away. Those tunes that are rare are valued. Therefore one should only transmit them when one has found the right man. I have lived for more than half

55   In the manuscript four lexigraphs have been rendered wholly or partly illegible from activity of bookworm. The passage reads as follows:[a]

金	谿	翫	花	石	季	倫	對	此	陶	興
1a	2a	3a	4a	5a	6a	7a	8a	9a	10a	11a

竹	林	勸	酣	阮	仲	容	彈	之	蕩	情
1b	2b	3b	4b	5b	6b	7b	8b	9b	10b	11b

者	也
(12	13)

From the strictly parallel structure it may be inferred that the characters 1a and 2a are part of the 'Studio-name' of Shi Chong, since characters 1b and 2b are part of the 'Studio-name' of Ruan Xian. Since Shi Chong's studio or estate was named 'Golden-valley'[50] the missing character (1a) is 'gold'.
The character 1b is clearly 'bamboo', as the surviving parts of the character show.
The nature of character 4b is evident from what remains: Radical 'Wine' on the left-hand side of the character, 'nine' on top of the right-hand side of the character, and a long down stroke on the bottom of the right-hand side suggest the full character 4b. This reading is supported by *Shishuo xinyu*, loc.cit[53]. Furthermore there is no other similar character in Chinese or Sino-japanese.

56   The pamphlet accompanying the facsimile of the manuscript[a] suggests Uda hō'ō[b] (who became a monk in 899) as the person indicated by Dajo hō'ō[c]. This seems probable, because Uda hō'ō was the father of Atsumi Shinnō[d] − 'the prince' in Sadayasu's manuscript − and this passage refers to the extraordinary musicality of the addressee's father, the retired emperor.

57   The title *Kōzuke no Taishu Shinnō*[a] refers to the son of Uda hō'ō, Atsumi Shinnō.

58   Sadayasu[a], the fourth son of Seiwa-tennō[b], was born on the 13th day of the 9th month in the 12th year of Jōgan[c]. His mother was Fujiwara Takako[d].
Sadayasu is one of the famous musicians of the period and was head of the Ceremonial Board in the second rank for princes[e]. He is referred to as the successor to Fujiwara Sadatoshi[f]. In addition to his fame as biwa-master, Sadayasu was even more famous for his flute-playing and as the compiler of the flute-scores Nanchikufu and Nangūfu[g]. He transcribed various pieces into horizontal flute notation. Conversely, he adapted for notched, vertical flute, shakuhachi[h] a version of the Tang-music piece Wang Zhaojun/Ōshōkun for horizontal flute, teki[i].
The only known reference to a teacher of Sadayasu cites Kobe Haruchika[j]. From the Japanese sources, we can only deduce with certainty that Kobe taught the flute.

a century, and it is hard to know how long [it will be before] I depart for the Ninth Spring[59]. If my life should suddenly come to an end, like the dew of the [Wu-] Tong tree[60], forthwith it will be dried up. I fear that these pieces and preludes will be scattered with the wind blowing through the pines[61], and will be lost for ever. The way makes no distinction between great and small, I am only concerned that it should not fall into oblivion. The number of all preludes is very great. I therefore wish to transmit entirely the secret techniques embodied in them. Begun at the time of the first winter month of the twentieth year of Engi, finished in the last autumn month of the twenty-first year [Engi][62].

The Prince[57] is by nature quick witted. Hearing one point he grasps ten. If he should live again, he will be reborn as a Boya[63] and will be immortal. Comparing him with the Weaving Damsel[64], the difference between them is less than the width of a needle. Respectfully, I now offer these tablatures to my Prince[57]. Alas! It is rare to encounter one would truly understands the heart of music, as the ancients lamented. I wrote down the chain of events as notes for future reference.

[59]   The Ninth Spring[a] refers to the underworld, viewed in a way similar to Dante's Nine Circles of the underworld[b].

[60]   *Sterculia platanifolia*; the wood of the *wutong-tree*[a] is primarily used for the making of musical instruments, especially for the qin, because of its good resonance. The most famous description of the wutong-tree occurs in Xi Kang, 'Poetical Essay on the Zither'[b]. In a Taoist context, as here, the idea of the wutong-tree also suggests a connection with the Red-Coral tree, the tree of the fruit of Immortality[c].

[61]   Tao Hongjing[a] spent his life in alchemical researches and in practising breathing techniques, supposed by Taoists to be conducive to immortality. He had his courtyard planted with pines, so that he could combine natural and human music, joining in with his lute when the wind swept through the fir-trees:
He particularly liked the wind in the pines. He planted pines in all court-yards, and when he heard their soughing enjoyed it and played music.[b]

[62]   We can deduce from the context, that the surviving copy of the manuscript was written for Atsumi Shinnō by Sadayasu. Sadayasu's being instructed in the contents of the manuscript had perhaps occurred just before (or after) he became Head of the Ceremonial Board. Sadayasu wrote the manuscript at the end of his life in the years 920-1 (Engi[a] 20-21) 'as a lasting record'.

[63]   *Boya*[a] was a famous legendary musician, carried to the Isles of the Blest by his teacher, so that his musical sense might be improved. His playing evoked images of hills and mountains, such that his listeners saw Taishan[b] rise before their eyes.

[64]   The 'Weaving Damsel'[a] is the star Vega in the constellation of Lyra[b]. The legend to which this passage refers was retold by R.Wilhelm[c]. The point of this cryptic reference is perhaps to compare Atsumi with a heavenly being[d] and to predict his immortality as a bright star.

琵琶譜序

夫琵琶者馬上之樂也形法三才絃

象四時飛鑑聽於秦年流妙曲於

漢曰公主之向烏孫綏　兵絕城之志

貂昌之辭鳳闕慰其遠嫁之悲

黢歔花石季倫討此陶興竹林勸首

阮仲容彈之蕩情者也太上法皇以

此器慶躁靜之中執踈密之要

勅上野太守親王就余學其音曲伏

惟物以秘為貴故待價深藏音以希

覓重故得人乃傳余百年之半已過九

Plate 2: Preface (FBBF, sheet 1)

137

泉之別離知君我生涯與桐露而忽
晞恐彼曲調混於風而長絶道無大小
只恐不墜凡厥調子數已繁多其中秘
手皆悉傳授始自延喜廿年孟冬終于
廿一年季秋親王天性洞曉聞一知十縱
令未生再生伯牙不死比之天孫間不容
鍼今以此譜奉度我到嗟乎知音難逢
古人所歎聊叙由緣以爲後日之張本而已

Plate 3: Preface continued (FBBF, sheet 2)

[39](a) The history of the lute in China has been studied extensively. For a bibliography and summary of researches see M. Gimm, *op.cit.*, p. 314 and pp. 305-410.

[40](a) 譜

(b) For a general introduction to tablatures see W. Apel, '*The Notation of Polyphonic Music 900-1600*', (Cambridge, Mass., 1953), pp 54-81; *Riemann Musiklexikon*, Sachteil (Mainz 1967), p. 931b and bibliography given there; for the Chinese term *pu* see *Yinyue zidian* 音樂字典 , (Taipeh 1963), p. 461b; M. Gimm, *op.cit.*, pp. 465-9, p. 631.

[41](a) 馬上樂

(b) *Jiu Tangshu* 舊唐書 , ch. 29, ed. Kaiming shudian 開明書店 (henceforth KM), vol. 4, p. 3178a; see also *Tang huiyao* 唐會要 , ch. 33, ed. Guoxue jiben congshu 國學基本叢書 (henceforth GXJBCS) 083-6, p. 621.

(c) 鮮卑

(d) 吐谷渾

(e) 部落稽

[42](a) 易經 ; R. Wilhelm, *I Ging* (Jena 1923), vol. 1, pp. 197 ff.

(b) 天

(c) 土

(d) 人

(e) 風俗通義

(f) cit. *Taiping yulan* 太平御覽 ch. 583, ed. Shanghai 1936, pp. 2b-3a.

[43](a) 四時 ; see *Yijing*, R. Wilhelm, *op.cit.*, vol. 2, pp. 1 f.; also *Liji* 禮記 ed. Sibu beiyao 四部備要 (henceforth SBBY) ch. 49, p. 17b, J. Legge, *The Liki*, (Reprint Taipeh 1961), vol. 2, pp. 465 ff.

139

44(a) Piba fu 琵琶賦 , ed. Jinding quan tangwen 欽定全唐文 ,
ch. 138, p. 3b.

(b) Yu Shinan 虞世南 558-638, biographies in *Jiu Tangshu,* ch. 72, ed. KM
p. 3322b; *Xin Tangshu* 新唐書, ch. 102, ed. KM p. 3917; short biography in Herbert
A. Giles, *A Chinese Biographical Dictionary* (Reprint Taipeh 1968) (henceforth Giles
BD) No. 2529.

(c) 秦

(d) 漢

45(a) Fu Xuan 傅玄 ?-278: biographies in *Hou Hanshu* 後漢書 ch. 50, ed.
KM p. 0740a; *Jinshu* 晉書 ch. 47, ed. KM p. 1209c; Giles BD No. 586.

(b) Du Zhi 杜摯 ?-263; biography in *Weishu* 魏書 ch. 21, ed. KM p. 0980c.

(c) Fu Xuan, Piba fu, ed. Quan Shang gu sandai qin han sanguo liuchao wen 全上
古三代秦漢三國六朝文 , ch. 45, p. 6a. Corresponding
quotations are in *Chuxue ji* 初學記 , ch. 16, ed. Peking 1962, vol 2, p. 392
et al. For a discussion of the origin of the Chinese lute see L. E. R. Picken, The origin
of the short lute, *The Galpin Society Journal*, vol 8 (1955), pp. 32-34;
L. E. R. Picken, T'ang music and musical instruments, *T'oung Pao*, vol. 55 (1969),
p. 108.

47(a) 烏孫 . See the commentary to *Qian Hanshu* 前漢書 ch. 66b, ed. GXJBCS
382-42, p. 5493 f.; G. Haloun, Zur Ue-tsi Frage, *Zeitschrift der Deutschen
Morgenländischen Gesellschaft* (henceforth ZDMG) 91 (1937), pp. 252 ff.;
O. Franke, *Geschichte des Chinesischen Reiches*, vol. 1, (Berlin 1930), pp. 341 ff.,
vol. 3 (Berlin 1937), pp. 187, 300 et al.; H. W. Haussig, Die Beschreibung des
Tarimbeckens bei Ptolemaios, ZDMG 109 (1959), p. 164, footnote;
E. G. Pulleyblank, Chinese and Indo-Europeans, *Journal of the Royal Asiatic Society*
(1966), pp. 9-39, especially p. 29 with f.n. 4.

(b) 天山

(c) See A. Herrmann, *An Historical Atlas of China*, (Edinburgh 1966), p. 11-D2,
p. 19-D3.

48(a) Wudi 武帝 156-87 BC; Giles BD No. 1276.

(b) Chang Qian 張騫 ?-114 BC; biographies in *Shiji* 史記 ch. 123, ed. KM
p. 0267a; *Qian Hanshu* ch. 61, ed. KM p. 0509c; Giles BD No. 29.

140

(c) 匈奴 ; see for a general account H. Franke und R. Trauzettel, *Das Chinesische Kaiserreich,* (Frankfurt am Main 1968), pp. 83 ff.

(d) Yuanfeng 元封 (110-105 BC); according to the *Zizhi tongjian* 資治通鑑 ch. 21, ed. Taipeh 1950, pp. 143a-b more precisely in the year 105 BC.

(e) 細君

(f) 江都王建

(g) Kunmo or Kunmi 昆莫 (昆彌), the king of the *Wusun*; for the meaning of the ending *-mi* in Central Asian context of the time see E. G. Pulleyblank, *op.cit.*[47a], pp.9-39. Acordingly to an unpublished article on the origin of the Central Asian state of the Central Asian state of the *Ruanruan* 蠕蠕 by L. Vajda and R. M. Wolpert the title Khan or qaghan as used in previous articles for Kunmo is first mentioned in *Beishi* 北史 ch. 98.

(h) Translation of the poem in A. Forke, *Blüten chinesischer Dichtung* (Magdeburg 1899), p. 10.

(i) *Qian Hanshu*, ch. 96b, ed. GXJBCS 382-42, p. 5497.

(j) See B. Watson, *Records of the Grand Historian*, (New York 1961), vol. 2, pp. 227 f.

(k) *Zizhi tongjian* ch. 27, p. 184c.

(l) See f.n. 43 above; M. Gimm *op.cit.*, p. 305 and pp. 320-22, f.n. 15; L. E. R. Picken, *loc.cit.*

[49](a) 王昭君

(b) Yuandi 元帝 , who ruled between 48 and 32 BC; see Giles BD No. 1350.

(c) Wangming jun ci 王明君詞 , *Wenxuan* 文選 ch. 27, ed. GXJBCS 177-6, p. 44.

(d) Wendi 文帝 , Sima Zhao 司馬昭 ; Giles BD No. 1746.

(e) Translation in E. Ritter von Zach, *Sinologische Beiträge II* (Batavia 1935), reprinted in *Die Chinesische Anthologie* (Cambridge, Mass. 1958), vol. 1, pp. 485 ff.

(f) By Liu Xin 劉歆 , First century BC and AD; Giles BD No. 1304.

(g) Wang Qiang 王嬙 in *Xijing zaji* 西京雜記 , ed. Sibu congkan, ch. 2, p. 1a. A paraphrase of the anecdote is to be found in Liu Jeng-en, *Six Yuan Plays*, (Harmondsworth 1972), pp. 32-3.

(h) The Yuan opera on the subject of Wang Zhaojun is entitled 'Hangong qiu 漢宮 秋 Autumn in the Han Palace', by Ma Zhiyuan 馬至遠 (1250?-1320?), in *Yuan quxuan* 元曲選 , ed. Peking 1958, p. V and 1 of the first volume.

(i) Tōgaku 唐樂

(j) See H. Eckardt, *Das Kokonchomonshū des Tachibana Narisue als musikgeschichtliche Quelle, Göttinger Asiatische Forschungen*, vol. 6 (Wiesbaden 1956), p. 130, f.n. 16 (on Sadayasu-no Miko).

(k) *Wuxian pu/Gogen-fu* 五絃譜 (commonly known as the *Gogenkin-fu* 五絃琴譜), dated 842; Yōmei-Bunko, formerly the private library of the Konoe family. See Hayashi Kenzō, Kokuhō gogenkinfu to sono kaitoku no tansho 國寶 五絃譜とその解読の端緒 , *Gagaku* (Tokyo 19), p. 138 ff. See also my study 'The tablature for five-stringed lute', in *Lute Music and Tablatures of the Tang Period.* (Ph.D. dissertation, University of Cambridge 1975).

[50](a) Jingu 金谷

(b) Instead of the character 谷 for 'valley' the manuscript gives the character with the same meaning.

(c) 金谷園

(d) *Shishuo xinyu* 世説新語 ch. c, ed. Taipeh 1969 (Zhong-guo xueshu mingzhi 中國學術名著 , section 1, vol. 154), pp. 550-7; a paraphrase of these anecdotes is given in W. Eichhorn, 'Zur Chinesischen Kulturgeschichte des 3. und 4. Jahrhunderts', ZDMG 91,2 (1937), pp. 475-6.

[51](a) Shi Chong 石崇 , style: Jilun 季倫 (249-300); biography in *Jinshu*, ch. 33, ed. KM p. 1177d, translated by H. Wilhelm in 'Shih Ch'ung and his Chin-ku-yuan', *Monumenta Serica* 18 (1959), pp. 314-27.

(b) Xi Jin 西晉 dynasty (265-313).

(c) See H. Wilhelm, *op.cit.*, p. 318.

(d) See M. Gimm, *op.cit.*, p. 307 and pp. 326 f. (f.n. 22); also *Jizuan yuanhai* 記纂 淵海 ch. 78, ed. 1579, p. 33b:

'Shi Jilun was outstanding in piba-playing.'
He was also the author of the poem Wangming jun zi[49c].

142

[52](a) Zhulin　竹林

(b) For the reconstruction of the sentence see f.n. 55.

(c) Zhulin qixian 竹林七賢 . Zhulin is in fact a geographical name, as shown in

R. H. van Gulik's, *Hsi K'ang and his poetical essay on the lute*, (Tokyo 1941), p. 13 f.n.; see also D. Holzmann, 'Les sept sages des forêt des bambous', *T'oung Pao* 44 (1956), p. 328.

[53](a) Liu Ling 劉伶 , third century AD; Giles BD No. 1328.

(b) R. H. van Gulik, *op.cit.*[52C], p. 14.

(c) According to *Shishuo xinyu*, ch. b., p. 268.

[54](a) Ruan Xian 阮咸 , style: Zhongyong 仲容 , third century AD; biography in

Jinshu, ch. 49, ed. KM p. 1214c; see also *Zhulin qixian xuanji* 竹林七賢選集 ,

(Hong Kong 1972) p. 42 ff.; He Bimin 何碧民 , *Zhulin qixian yanjiu* 竹林七

賢研究 , (Taipeh 1964) p. 39-44.

(b) Ruan Ji 阮籍 (210-36); Giles BD. No. 2544 (the correct reading of the

family-name is Ruan, not Yuan as given in Giles BD.) M. Gimm, *op.cit.*, p. 327 ff mistakenly refers to Ruan Xian as the son of Ruan Ji. See Ruan Xian's biography, *loc.cit.*, and *Shishuo xinyu*, ch. b, p. 268.

(c) Yinlü 音律

(d) *Jinshu, loc.cit.*; his extraordinary abilities as a musician are also referred to in *Beitang*

shuchao 北堂書鈔 , ch. 110, ed. 1888, p. 3b; *Yiwen leiju* 藝文

類聚 ch. 44, ed. Taipeh 1960, p. 8a; *Jiu Tangshu*, ch. 29, ed. KM p. 3178d;

Tongdian 通典 , ch. 144, ed. Taipeh 1969, p. 753b; for a translation of the

Tongdian passage, see M. Gimm, *op.cit.*, p. 329.

[55](a) See plate, p. 137

(b) Compare Morohashi Tetsuji 諸橋轍次 , *Dai Kan-wa jiten* 大漢

和辞典 , Tokyo -1960, vol. 13 (Index).

[56](a) *Fushiminomiya-bon biwa-fu kaidai*

(b) Uda hō'ō 宇多法皇

(c) 太上法皇

[57](a) 上野太守新王

[58](a) 貞保（新王）

(b) 清和天皇 (851-881)

(c) Twelfth year of Jōgan 貞觀 (870).

(d) 藤原高子

(e) Nihon shikibukyō 二品式部卿

(f) Fujiwara Sadatoshi 藤原貞敏 , see postface, p. 149, and f.n. See also *Ryūmeishō* 龍鳴抄 , ed. Gunsho Ruijū, vol 19, p. 41; *Kyōkunshō* 教訓抄 ,ed. Zoku-Gunsho Ruijū, vol. 19, p. 323; *Kaichiku shō* 懷竹抄 ed. Gunsho Ruijū, vol. 19, p. 77; *Taigenshō* 體原鈔 , ed. Nihon koten Zenshū, maki 5, ed. Tokyo 1933, p. 550.

(g) *Nanchikufu* 南竹譜 and *Nangufu* 南宮譜 .

(h) Shakuhachi 尺八 (i) teki 笛

(j) Kobe (or ?Furube) Haruchika 古部春近 , see *Taigenshō*, maki 5, p. 558; H. Eckardt, *loc.cit.*

[59](a) Jiuyan 九原 ; other versions are jiuquan 九泉 , jiujing 九京 , and huangyuan 黄原 . See H. Franke, Die Geschichte des Prinzen Tan von Yen', ZDMG 107 (1957), p. 429; W. Bauer und H. Franke, *Die Goldene Truhe* (München 1959), p. 26 and p. 427.

(b) See R. A. Stein, 'L'Habitat, le monde et le corps humain en extrème-orient et en haute asie', *Journal Asiatique* vol. 245 (1957), pp. 37-74.

[60](a) Wutong-tree 梧桐木 ; for the relation – or non-relation – of trees in China called 'tong' see E. H. Schafer, *The Golden Peaches of Samarkand*, Los Angeles (1963), p. 186.

(b) Xi Kang 嵇康 , *Qinfu* 琴賦 , ed. Quan Sanguo wen 全三國文 , ch. 47, p. 1b; Translations by E. Ritter von Zach, *op.cit.*, p. 251 ff.; R. H. van Gulik, *op.cit.*[52C], especially p. 74 and p. 82.

(c) Cetong, *Erythrina indica*, see B. Laufer, *Sino-Iranica*, Publication 204, Anthropological ̓Series, vol. 15, No. 3, Field Museum of Natural History (Chicago 1919), p. 478, f.n. 1; E. H. Schafer, *loc.cit.*; for the connection with the fruit for immortality, see Qu Yuan 屈原 , Lisao 離騷 , ed. GXJBCS 199-1, p. 11; P. Weber-Schäfer, *Altchinesische Hymnen* (Köln 1967), p. 208 and p. 194.

[61](a) Tao Hongjing 陶弘景 (451-536); biographies in *Nanshi* 南史 ch. 76, ed. KM p. 2725a; Giles BD No. 1896.

(b) *Nanshi, loc.cit.*

[62](a) Twentieth and twenty-first year Engi 延喜 (920-1)

[63](a) 伯牙 ; Giles BD No. 1662.

(b) 太山

[64](a) Tiansun 天孫

(b) *Qian Hanshu*, ch. 6, ed. GXJBCS 382-17, p. 2194.

(c) R. Wilhelm, 'Der Kuhirte und die Spinnerin', in *Chinesische Märchen* (Köln 1952), pp. 32-5.

(d) Tiansun was one of the seven daughters of the King of Heaven.

COLOPHON

In the third year of Kaicheng of the Great Tang, in the fifth year of the cycle, in the eighth month, on the seventh day, the twenty-ninth day of the cycle[65], the Japanese official made a petition and gave it to Wang Yuzhen[66] who held the position of Yinjing guanglu dafu[67] and was in the nominal rank of Taizi shushi[68], respectfully asking the Yangchow Regional Commission[69] for a piba-master[70].

In the same year, in the ninth month, seventh day, the fifty-ninth day of the cycle, in accordance with the petition, they sent a Master, Lian Chengwu[71] (style: Shiqi; age: eighty-five years) of the First Division of the Provincial Administration[72].

Whereupon, at the Water-Inn north of the Kaiyüan temple[73], he taught practical exercises and modal preludes. In the same month, on the twenty-ninth day, when proficiency in the art was reached, Master Lian Chengwu sent this tablature as a lasting record.

[65] Third year Kaicheng 開 成 (838)

[66] According to Ennin's diary a petition was handed over to Wang Yuzhen[a]* on the ninth day of the eighth month 838:
> The commissioner in charge of the Japanese Embassy, Wang Yuzhen came to the official inn.[b]

* Secondary footnotes are given on p. 148.

[67] Yinjing guanglu dafu[a], Civil Ranking Officer in the tank IIIb[b].

[68] Taizi shushi[a], the crownprince's nobleman.

[69] Guan chafu[a], 'Un commissaire impérial a la surveillance (d'un region)[b]'

[70] piba boshi

[71] A piba-player Lian Jiao[a] is mentioned elsewhere[b] as the highest ranking piba-player at the court of the then governor of Yangchow, Li Deyu[c]. Lian Chengwu[d] was either the same person as Lian Jiao or a near relative. Lian Jiao's teacher was a certain Cao Gang[e], probably a musician from Kabudhan[f]. The following genealogy for the tradition of piba-playing preserved in FBBF is suggested:
> Cao Gang – Lian Jiao/Lian Chengwu – Fujiwara Sadatoshi – anonymous pupil of Sadatoshi/Teacher of Sadayasu – Sadayasu Shinnō (-Atsumi Shinnō).

In later Japanese sources, Lian Chengwu plays an important role as the ancestor of Japanese biwa-playing[g]. Some of the statements made in these (later) Japanese sources are legendary only, or misleading; for instance, the report that Renshobu (=Lian Chengwu) taught Fujiwara Sadatoshi in the second year of Jōwa (835)[h]. This statement is contradicted by the fact, that the Japanese embassy did not reach China until 838, and by the date given in the colophon to FBBF. This has led to the suggestion, by scholars who do not know of the existence of FBBF[i], that Lian Chengwu was only a mythical figure.

[72] This refers to the court of Li Deyu, Governor of Yangchow.

[73] See also Ennin's diary:
> The minister of state (that is, Li Deyu) arranged a farewell banquet at the Water-Inn for the envoys going to the capital.[a]

Recorded in the third year of Kaicheng, in the ninth month, on the twenty-ninth day, by the Administrative Officer, Fujiwara Sadatoshi[74].

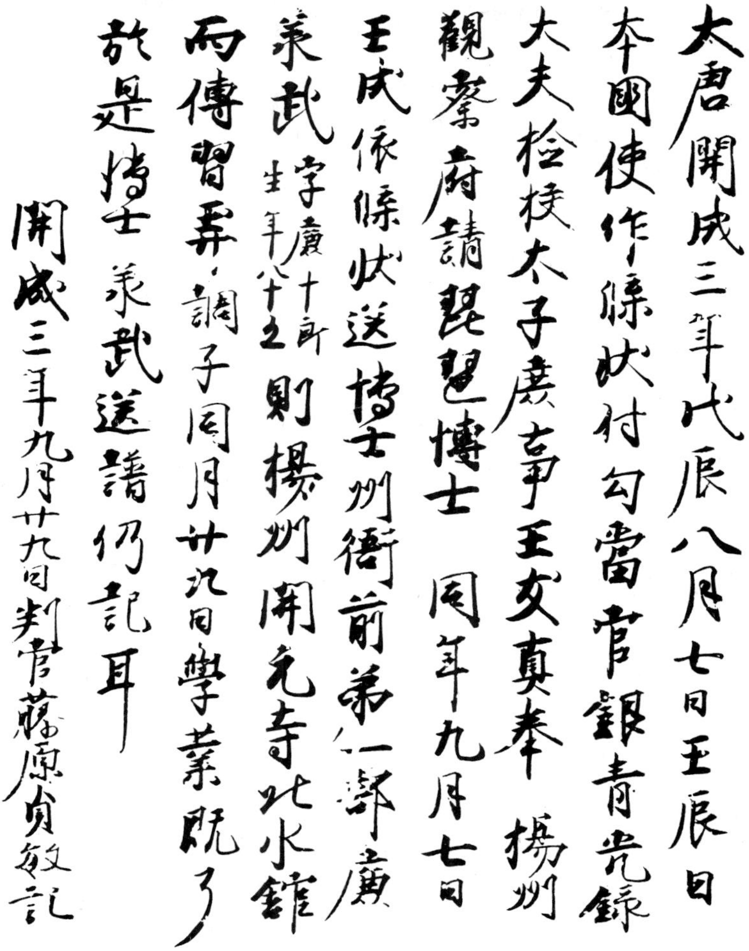

太唐開成三年代辰八月七日壬辰日
本國使作條狀付勾當官銀青光錄
大夫捡挍太子廣亭王玄真奉　揚州
觀察府請琵琶博士　同年九月七日
王成依條狀送博士州衙前第八部廣
兼武　字廣十所　生年廿二　則揚州開元寺北水館
丙傳習弄　調子同月廿九日學業既了
敢是博士　兼武送譜仍記耳
開成三年九月廿九日判官藤原貞敏記

Plate 4: Colophon (FBBF, sheet 24)

[74] Fujiwara Sadatoshi[a] lived between 807 and 867, and was an Administrative Officer of the Japanese Embassy to China in 834-841.[b]

147

[66](a) 王友真

(b) *Nittō guhō junrei gyoki-no kenkyū* (Tokyo 1964), vol. 1, p. 176; translation in E. O. Reischauer, *Ennin's Diary, The Record of a Pilgrimage to China in Search of the Law*, (New York 1955), p. 28.

[67](a) Yinjing guanglu dafu　銀青光錄大夫　, Civil Ranking Officer, IIIb; see the table appended to *Shina toshi* Tokyo 1942, vol. 2.

[68](a) Taizi shushi　太子庶事　, see *Tongdian* ch. 30, p. 171a-b.

[69](a) Guan chafu　觀察府

(b) R. des Retours, *Traité des fonctionaires et traité de l'armée*, (Leiden 1947-8), vol. 2, p. 669.

[71](a) Lian Jiao　廉郊

(b) *Yuefu zalu*; see M. Gimm, *op.cit.*, p. 310 and f.n. 149, pp. 383-5.

(c) See M. Gimm, *loc.cit.*, and f.n. 147, p. 382 f.

(d) Lian Chengwu　廉承武

(e) Cao Gang　曹綱　, see M. Gimm, *loc.cit. et al.*

(f) Caoguo; E. Chavannes, *Documents sur les Tou-Kiue (Turcs) occidentaux* (St. Petersburg 1903) p. 139.

(g) See *Kojidan*　古事談　, ed. Kokushi Taikei, XV, maki 6, p. 138, *Sandai-jitsuroku*　三代實錄　, Seiwa-tennō, Jogan ninth year (867), 10th month, fourth day; *Jikkinshō*　十訓抄　, ed. Jikkinshō-shokai (S. Ishibashi), maki 10, 19, p. 451.

(h) *Bunkidan* 文机談　, maki 2, p. 19; see H. Eckardt, *op.cit.*, p. 133.

(i) H. Eckardt, *loc.cit.*; E. Harich-Schneider, *A History of Japanese Music*, (London 1973), P. 101.

[73](a) *Nittō guhō junrei gyoki-no kenkyū,* vol. 1, p. 224; E. O. Reischauer, *op.cit.*, p. 41.

[74](a) 藤原貞敏

(b) See *Rikkokushi*　六國史　, *Sandai-jitsuroku, loc.cit.*; M. Gimm, *op.cit.*, p. 384; E. Harish-Schneider, *op.cit.*, p. 261; H. Eckardt, *op.cit.*, p. 132 ff.; W. Adriaansz, *The Kumiuta and Danmono Traditions of Japanese Koto Music* (Los Angeles 1973), p. 4. The statement that Sadatoshi was a blind biwa-player is certainly wrong; it reflects unconsciously the *topos* of 'The Blind Musician', common both in the West and in East Asia.

SUMMARY STATEMENT OF CONTENT OF PREFACE AND COLOPHON

The preface consists of three parts, all in Chinese. The first gives the standard *topoi* for the piba in Chinese texts of the Tang period, similar to those in Duan Anjie's *Piba lu*, for example. The sequence of allusions to the Wusun-Princess, to Wang Zhaojun, to Shi Chong and to Ruan Xian, already standardized in early *piba fu* (on which, in turn, most encyclopedias are based), amounts to a somewhat shortened version of the standard 'history' of the lute in China. This part of the preface is of a piece with other Tang literature on musical instruments. The second and third parts of the preface were probably written by Prince Sadayasu (870-924). The third part is an appraisal of the abilities of his pupil, Prince Atsumi, again referring to topoi in Chinese mythology. Remarkable are the frequent allusions to Taoism and Taoists. It is known that the lute played an important role in shamanistic and folk-religious rites in Central and East Asia; for example, in the invocation of rain-making spirits[75].

In the first part of the preface, two of the four persons mentioned by name, Shi Chong and Ruan Xian, have Taoist connections. The latter is often attributed with the 'invention' of a 'new' type of lute, the *ruan*, named after its 'inventor'.

In the second part of the preface, the text alludes to the Wutong-tree, the wood of which is important in the making of musical instruments, in particular, the qin. The tree is also a symbol of immortality in Chinese mythology and in particular in Taoist contexts, as described in Xi Kang's *Qinfu*. Both Xi Kang and Ruan Xian were musicians in the group of the 'Seven Sages of (the) Bamboo-grove' of the third century AD.

An allusion to music merging with the wind in the pines recalls the famous Taoist and alchemist, Tao Hongjing, who sought immortality both by the preparation of alchemical elixirs (*waidan*), and by the regulation of heartbeat and the breathing techniques of 'minor alchemy (*neidan*)'. He had his courtyard planted with pines, so that he might combine natural and human music by joining the sound of his lute with that of the wind sweeping through the trees. In pre-Tang texts, Tao Hongjing was reported to play the zither, qin, but by Tang times the allusion is nearly always to his playing the lute. This had become the musical instrument of the non-Confucian literati. An allusion to the various ways of gaining immortality, and to uncertainty about the correct way, occurs perhaps in the reference to the Way, that is 'neither great nor small'. This may indicate that Taoist *neidan* and *waidan* techniques were no longer integral to one school (as in pre-Tang times), but had already begun to diverge — a division well-eshablished in Sung times. Allusions to immortality also occur in the third part of the preface: to Boya[63], and to the 'Weaving Damsel'[64], one of the Seven Daughters of the King of Heaven, who married a mortal and subsequently became a star (as did her husband).

---

[75] See R. F. Wolpert, Einige Bemerkungen zur Geschichte des Streichinstruments in China, *Central Asiatic Journal,* vol. XVIII (1974), p. 259, and f.n. 35.

The preface, as we have it then, is probably a conflation of the original preface (in whole or in part), written by Lian Chengwu, with second and third parts, written by Prince Sadayasu. It makes typically Chinese allusions to Taoism, and in doing so strengthens the thesis that a close relationship existed between Taoism (*Daojiao* 道 教) and the lute. It enables us to date FBBF as a copy of an original manuscript, brought from China by Fujiwara Sadatoshi (see also colophon), where he was taught piba by Lian Chengwu, a musician at the court of Li Deyu at Yangchow. The copy was written in 920-1 by Sadayasu Shinnō when over fifty years of age.

TRANSCRIPTION OF THE MODAL PRELUDES

The modal preludes transcribed below are followed by the statement:

'For oral transmission only'.

thus qualifying the preludes as part of the 'secret repertory' of Japanese court music[76].

> 'Now concerning these modal preludes: according to the Tang notation, one presses only at one fret and plays it; according to the teachings of the Master, one strikes, adding many strings, and plays it. Again, in Tang notations, there are few ornamental notes; in the Teachings of the Master, there are many ornamental notes. In addition, in this score, there are tuning pieces for all modes.'[77]

The modal preludes preserved in FBBF probably reflect both performing practice and modal preludes known in China well before the compilation of the original manuscript in 838. This is suggested by two facts. As stated in the colophon of FBBF, the teacher of the original addressee, Fujiwara Sadatoshi, namely Lian Chengwu, was already 85 years of age when he transmitted the modal preludes to his Japanese pupil. Yet more striking is the fact that the single, short modal prelude preserved in Tempyō[7] was included, by Lian Chengwu, in his collection, even though the latter was compiled probably one hundred years after Tempyō was written[78]. In the following transcriptions Tempyō has been compared with the later versions of FBBF and SGYR.

The statement on playing practice (translated above) indicates the first Japanese changes in the repertory imported from China, namely, the addition of open-string chords and ornamental notes[79].

---

[76]   See H. Eckardt, *op.cit.*, p. 133 et al.

[77]   FBBF, sheet 15, lines 9-12.

[78]   Tempyō is written on the back of a document of the year Tempyō 19 or 20 (747 or 748).

[79]   The development of Tang-music into Tōgaku will be discussed in a later study. Note the important statement, that the playing is different, but the notation remains unchanged.

The statement also implies, however, use of the bachi (the plectrum used for biwa-playing). But the bachi, though mentioned in FBBF, was certainly not used for the modal preludes. Apart from the right-hand *fingering* indicated in the last two preludes, the fact that a bachi was not used may also be deduced from the fact that notated chords, in other preludes, make use of notes on non-consecutive strings (that is, with one or two unplucked strings between the strings to be plucked), a practice possible for the fingers but impossible for a plectrum.

Most of the modal preludes brought from China by Fujiwara Sadatoshi and preserved in FBBF are also incorporated in SGYR. This fact strongly supports the view that this Japanese Tōgaku manuscript for lute (SGYR) preserves Tang tunes as played in the ninth century at the latest.

In the following comparison of the versions of the two manuscripts: FBBF and SGYR, the reading of the modal preludes as preserved in FBBF is shown on the upper stave, that of SGYR on the lower. For easier reference, all modal preludes have been given serial numbers: The first (roman) numeral indicates the mode, the second (arabic) numeral the position of the prelude in the particular modal sequence:

I   Fengxiang tiao
II   Fan Fengxiang tiao
III   Huangzhong tiao.

I₁

*The second quaver from the end of this stave should be d.

153

154

I₄

II₁

156

158

160

end of fragment

Sheet missing in FBBF

163

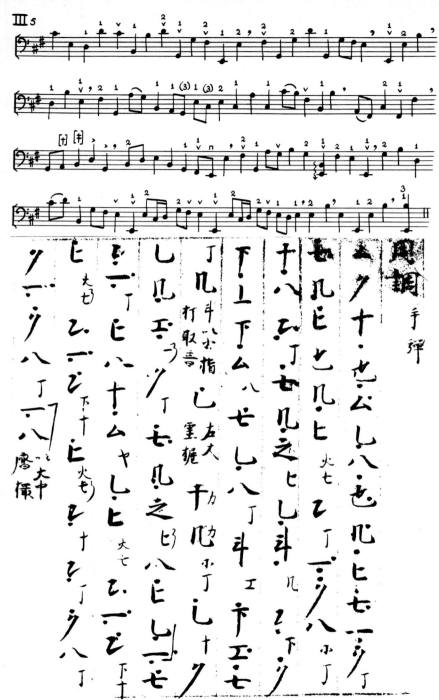

Plate 5: Fingered Modal Prelude in Huangzhong tiao (FBBF, sheet 12, lines 10-12; sheet 13, lines 1-7)

Notes to the transcription of Modal Preludes III, 4, 4a, and 5

*) Percuss [the string] with little finger to obtain note.

∗∗) Play note with the *gou*-movement [see p. 121] of the little finger.

§) Thumb and middle finger pluck the string together.

§§§) Play note with the *tiao*-movement [see p. 122] of the thumb.

†) Percuss with little finger to obtain note.

††) The thumb of the left hand plucks the string.

ACKNOWLEDGEMENTS

My greatest debt is to my teacher, Dr L. E. R. Picken, F.B.A., who has followed my work through all its stages. Dr R. K. Marlow has given invaluable help on musical problems, while sinological advice and encouragement have been received from Prof. D.C. Twitchett, F.B.A., and Prof. H. Franke (University of Munchen). To Prof. Fukushima Kazuo I am greatly indebted for the probable identification of 'the prince' mentioned in the preface to FBBF.

The research was financed by grants from the Bavarian Ministry of Culture (Graduiertenförderung), and from the Andrew Mellon Foundation.

This paper was written in 1974 when I was a research student at Jesus College, Cambridge.